Cont

I HAVE CONTROL...

First edition, published in 2000 by

WOODFIELD PUBLISHING
Woodfield House, Babsham Lane, Bognor Regis
West Sussex PO21 5EL, England.

ISBN 1-873203-51-9

I HAVE CONTROL

Humorous autobiographical observations of an ex-RAF Officer

EDWARD CARTNER

Woodfield Publishing

BOGNOR REGIS • WEST SUSSEX • ENGLAND

Introduction

When two pilots in the same aircraft hand over control of the machine from one to the other, a time-honoured mantra is invoked.

"You have control..." intones the first, taking his hands from the control column.

"I have control...", confirms the second...

And everybody in the aircraft must hope that it is so!

The late Colin Welch, respected columnist of *The Daily Telegraph*, is said to have answered the suggestion that events should be run with 'military precision' by quipping, "Have you ever been in the Army?" This was not to question the other's background, but rather to poke fun at that institution for which he held considerable affection.

As a military officer, giving those around you the impression that you are effortlessly in control is an essential part of the performance. However, like a serene swan that glides through swift currents with unruffled feathers, whilst out of sight it is thrashing around furiously to maintain its course, the outward insouciance of officers at junior level

– and probably those at a senior level too – frequently conceals matters only just under command.

Throughout my own military career, personal catastrophe often seemed just around the corner and only furious paddling could save my day; unfortunately, I often failed to paddle hard enough!

The anecdotes contained herein are of actual events – with mild embroidery – and mainly concern the Royal Air Force, but I feel sure that any sailor or soldier would also recognise the predicaments and pitfalls described.

EDWARD CARTNER
Plymouth, 2000

A Change of Life

~ 1 ~

A Change of Life

Nobody was fooled in 1964 when we RAF officer cadets assured our tutors that all we needed was earnest discussion on air power strategy followed by proud foot drill in emotional silence. The truth was that we could hardly wait to adopt our rank and then wow the girls in our new uniforms. Towards the end, however, an obstacle appeared. We learned that to many people our title on graduation could be *Mister*. *Mister?* I'd been a *Mister* as a schoolteacher. All right, nobody expected to become Squadron Leader Biggles overnight, but, I ask you, *Mister!* It appeared that only after winning our spurs and a promotion would we lose that title.

Our dismaying handle was confirmed by the arrival of that essential item, for those days, of all officers' accoutrement, the calling card. There on pure white pasteboard cut to regulation dimension, was the word *Mister* for all to read. During one astonishing lesson we learned to pass a finger nail surreptitiously over the face of a proffered card, feel the raised ink and thereby judge the social worth of the fellow before us. It seemed incredible that such a superficial layer of Dickensian conduct was to be laid upon us as we entered the most technically advanced service.

Amazingly, most of us survived this nonsense and were sent off to our first appointments. Carrying all my worldly goods in a large black tin trunk – I have it still – and anxiously running a finger tip over my own impeccable credentials, I arrived at my new station.

First call was to deposit two of the cards on a silver tray so that my commanding officer and colleagues could note my arrival in writing, as it were. It was the only ritual I recognised from training and within days faced unforeseen and baffling aspects of 'real' Air Force society. Officers were required to wear head dress at all times and it was not long before I was loudly and publicly instructed in personal deportment by an aggressive neighbour with a mission in life. Hatless, I was washing the car in my own front drive at the time. Later he introduced an over-glamorous woman with attitude who, in a gush of "Daaahlings", assumed command of my wife's modest wardrobe. Meanwhile, I had been summoned by the guard commander at the main gate to explain the arrival of an asthmatic car containing two cats and a cross female hippy sporting a gigantic CND badge. It was my sister who demanded entry to visit her "kid brother." Already I was wondering why I'd ever left the shelter of my former life.

Then a written directive required me to instruct my spouse – yes, *instruct* – that the commanding officer's lady would be 'at home' on certain afternoons. There she would cordially receive all newly-arrived wives with tea and small cake accompanied by refined probing into their antecedents. My wife would open her pack of calling cards for the first time – oh, yes, she had to have them too – and, via the Adjutant, deposit a card in advance thereby giving sufficient notice.

We had no children to impede our anxious preparations, so these amounted to an extra polish of the family car. This was a sit-up-and-beg Ford Popular, severely outdated even then and a most un-officer-like vehicle. Together with other wear and tear, it suffered from chronic blown valves which made for unpredictable starting.

On the morning of my wife's ordeal, I was self-consciously marching myself about the place in my brand-new brass-buttoned uniform when a long black car drew slowly alongside. It was an Alvis or a Lagonda or some such elegant make dating from the real days of calling cards. The driver was an imperious lady in an 'Ascot' hat who asked the way to the parade ground. As that was also my destination – to attend a passing-out ceremony – I invited myself on board to show the road. My recent training had laid only a thin layer of urbanity over a robust Northumbrian upbringing, but I uttered a froth of solicitous enquiries about her journey... Had she been here before? ... How lovely the weather was... All in an endless prattle giving no chance of response. So anxious was my attention that I missed the vital turn and directed her into a circuitous one-way maze and we were quickly lost.

She found her own way out, and parked the car at the proper place. I failed by a whisker to rush round and open her door, but my final shot was the epitome of old-style charm. "Have you met the Station Commander? His name is..."

"Indeed I have, Mister, er ... He is my husband."

I saw little point in fishing out a calling card.

During the afternoon my wife fared better than I. She arrived on time, handled the card trick with aplomb and, in the enviable way of women, made easy conversation with the great lady until she recognised the subtle signs of gracious dismissal.

It was quite extraordinary, after all, she'd had no training whatever.

Then fate took the stage. As the hostess waited in polite farewell, our aged car refused to start, no matter what. Eventually, house servants were called to push the thing until bangs and clouds of smoke announced imminent departure. By then the threshold was quite deserted.

At home that evening my wife and I compared notes. "I had a pretty good day," I began . "I escorted the CO's wife to the parade. How about you?"

"Not bad," she mused. "Darling, now that we've changed our lives, can we get a new car?"

And so we did.

However, although we never used our calling cards again, I remained *Mister* for a while longer.

I Surrender...
Dobby's in Charge

~ 2 ~

I Surrender...
Dobby's in Charge

In the early sixties it was perfectly normal for a young officer living in mess to have a batman appointed. What caught me by surprise was that the same privilege applied to those of us who occupied married quarters. Early morning call with a cup of tea and newly-polished shoes was never on the menu, but looking after the officer's kit certainly was. It was probably because authority considered that any penniless young man left in the care of his wife alone, would quickly find his lifestyle reduced to a sordid shambles requiring a minder to rectify matters. In my case, as I owned next to no domestic possessions, the 'batty' was simply keeping a beady eye on the Government property, myself included, which temporarily filled our house.

The theory in those days was that the servant man cared for the officer and his immediate accoutrements, but if a wife happened to be one of those, then her share of the quarter also received some attention in the nature of things.

Matters were more single-mindedly masculine in tone, so it occurred to no one, least of all me, that a woman, newly installed in her private, albeit Government-issue nest, might resent interference in her domain. Similarly, it never appeared at all odd to leave a pregnant young woman alone in the male company of a total stranger. We didn't even have a telephone.

Although in truth we were equally apprehensive about the whole business, a short commuting journey to my duty station saved me further pain and I left my wife one morning anxiously awaiting our first servant's arrival. She had dusted around and tidied up in preparation for the very person hired to do just that. We learned from new friends, with whom we shared the week's work, that such preparation was traditional.

It was to be some months before I actually set eyes on my batman, but became accustomed to an evening report following the weekly four-hour session of my entitlement.

"Gosh, he does drink a lot of tea," was an early comment. Then, "Do you notice any difference in the place?" she would ask.

I rarely did , but loyalty demanded poor comparison with her efforts.

Then I learnt of the character employed from an unidentified rehabilitation centre who spent his only session with us in a vain attempt to light the fire. This was a vital winter ritual in a big house with no central heating on top of a wind swept North-Yorkshire hill. My return one evening found my wife sitting moist-eyed, but passably warm beside the open kitchen oven burning at gas mark six. The batty's work for the day was indelibly recorded in spilled stove-black over the hearth rug and a trail of sooty finger prints from back to front. Every fire lighter block and that day's newspaper had been consumed. Of flames there was no sign.

Some mysterious bureaucracy intervened and, without cause by us, he was replaced by a gentle soul who quickly took a fancy to the many female bottles adorning our dressing table. My wife only discovered this one day when she stood close to him and smelt herself passing by as it were. She said that a surprise return by me had him gulping scalding coffee in his haste to return to work. It seemed that at every other house he was required to take his break in the garden outhouse and feared I would consider relaxing in the back kitchen a democratic step too far.

As was only proper, I had entered my quarters by the front and noticed nor smelt nothing unusual.

If the women had to learn by trial and error, it was hardly better for the men whose social training by and large comprised how to present calling cards, that officers should not carry parcels nor ever be seen in public without head dress. How to establish a convivial relationship between officer and man-servant seemed curiously absent.

After enduring our own trial by short-term oddballs, I was appointed to the care of a real 'batty' of the old school. He was called Dobby and friends warned, "Don't be fooled by his thick glasses. He's as blind as a bat, but misses nothing." Certainly he set-to with gusto and we enjoyed some weeks of diligence. My wife reported that he was most certainly in a different league to all others, so it seemed proper for me to come home one mid-morning, address my man and set the standards to be achieved.

After a Dobby morning the place was unrecognisable, our few brasses gleamed, domestic non-military clutter was tidied away as if for inspection and the well-laid fire ignited to a single match. We displayed a ceremonial sword on the hall table and its bright work and black leather scabbard became the principal target for Dobby's zeal. One day the weapon was missing. After a long search he found it under the marital bed where my wife had kept it for reassurance when alone in the house during a short duty absence of mine. It was triumphantly restored to the place of honour and his fearless Yorkshire scorn should have warned me.

So I stood in front of my own gleaming hearth and warmed my backside in the full majesty of the paterfamilias. If I'd worn a watch chain, I would have thrust my thumbs into it and patted my paunch. Our baby daughter, having just discovered feet, counted her toes and babbled softly in what we grandly called the nursery. Dobby worked upstairs while we took morning coffee from fine bone china. Then my wife went up to advise him that the master awaited and returned to sit demurely on the edge of her easy chair hands folded in her lap.

A regular flicking sound told of more non-existent dust being removed and then, with a pause to adjust the sword, a steady tread approached the drawing room. I straightened my expensively uniformed back and as if for comparison, thrust forward the glittering buttons polished by my own hand that very morning. It was to be a defining moment in my newly-acquired status as a leader of men.

Without knocking, I noted, an elderly figure dressed in a lightly starched brown dust-coat entered the room and peered at me through impossibly thick spectacle lenses. As if about to send a semaphore flag message, he carried a bright yellow duster in each hand. "This is Dobby," said my wife quietly.

"Ah, there you are, Dobby, my good man," I began graciously. "How do you like working in my house? You certainly achieve high standards."

With the pride and dignity of a regimental sergeant major he came close and subjected my turn-out to a withering inspection. My wife and I waited through a long pause until, in magnificent Yorkshire tones, he made it clear just who was in charge in that house.

"Aye, that I do," he snorted. "But what I'll do with you I don't know. In that bathroom I reckons you throw talcum powder up in t'air and just stand underneath like."

Never Volunteer

~ 3 ~

Never Volunteer

Newly appointed youngsters must strike a careful balance between safe anonymity and risky notoriety. Too mouse-like and superiors will simply not realise they exist. Too loud and thunderbolts a-plenty are attracted. Early, but complimentary notice by one's commanding officer is the aim.

My group was in the usual post-training limbo after successful graduation. Not experienced enough to merit credibility, yet anxious to make a mark of some sort. Our basic training had accustomed us to jumping out of aircraft with a static line or automatic parachute, but now we faced the frights of free-fall.

Health and Safety at Work complications seemed few and, although the training was comprehensive, the final safety brief boiled down to a robustly simple "Pull the handle, or die."

Earlier we had watched the nonchalant departure of the experts as they stepped out with mock salutes, grins and, for the more stylish, collars and ties. Their comfortable slide down the aircraft slipstream established the minimum requirement. At our turn we novices quickly failed to meet even our own low standards. A colleague's involuntary performance of a full Olympic gymnastic sequence, complete with tuck and half-twist, before passing under the aircraft tail-plane set a new target. After my jump I would claim a higher tariff by achieving two full twists as well as omitting 'Two', 'Three' and 'Four' of the intended calm count of five seconds. I simply gasped 'One. Five. PULL!'

There would be sarcastic trouble from my instructor on landing, but for the time being, suspended at about two and a half thousand feet beneath a glorious candy-striped parachute, I was untouchable. The immediate task was simply to steer into a field at least a mile square.

Instead, in a glowing exaltation of continued life, but total inactivity, I hung like a rag doll and watched the distant green pass below my boots. This was followed by a hedge, a ploughed field, another hedge and then a copse of trees. Into the topmost branches of this I arrived in a shower of twigs and outraged rooks.

Above me a melody of expensive-sounding rips told of the parachute's snagging and my whimpering progress came to a yo-yo halt. I hung between two trunks each just beyond reach, but still 20 feet or so up.

The subsequent recovery is too embarrassing to relate in detail. Suffice it to say that a member of the ground party shinned up and lowered me like a sack of potatoes. Then there was a ruined parachute, a contemptuous farmer whose low opinion of the military had been amply reinforced and eventually, a felled tree to recover the tatters.

Now I was out of the herd. My name was on everybody's lips and I must surely be known to my commanding officer. I'd broken out of the anonymous ranks, a glittering career could only follow.

During the curiously one-sided discussion which followed my heroic demonstration, the boss took a telephone call. His eyes lit up and I knew at once who was the subject of the call.

"Short-notice weekend duty? No problem. I'll let you have that bloody idiot who got stuck up a tree. You know the one. Er..." He looked towards me. "What's your name?"

Well Above The Salt

~ 4 ~

Well Above The Salt

From my lofty, but unaccustomed position on the 'top table' of a formal dinner night, I had to agree that the perspective was different. The normal place for juniors of my lowly rank was at the foot of the table well removed from the leaders. Tonight from a lonely eminence I could just see my friends through the glare of the candles as they indulged in the normal below-the-salt noisy banter.

Other than a conventional greeting when taking our seats, my dining neighbours had immediately turned away to their peers on either hand for high-rank gossip and other worldly affairs. Clearly, I was expected to contribute little so had to content myself with careful table manners and precise timing of knife and fork in step with my betters. It was certain that I would be returned abruptly to the pits on the next occasion.

Towards the centre of the table a senior guest sat at the favoured place beside my station commander and with relaxed conversation fitted in with ease. I took consolation by remembering that it was me who had introduced him to the mess and so, it appeared, given my commander something refreshingly different to talk about. It was a satisfying social coup for a young man and no doubt I would soon be congratulated on my choice.

Some weeks earlier in accordance with established procedure and as specified in the book, I had written a formal submission to the Mess President for permission to introduce my guest. He was a civilian, but I was confident that he would manage the ritual of a formal military dinner without any problem. He would be staying in my house over the date and very much looked forward to the occasion.

On the day before the dinner I received a gracious agreement to my request. My guest would appear on the seating plan well down the pecking order, but, and in accordance with normal practice, close to his host and therefore the other juniors. Meanwhile, for the interest of the station commander, who would offer all guests a public welcome, I was to produce by cease work short biographical notes.

So far all perfectly normal.

Towards midday of the following day I was summoned by my immediate commander. The meeting began without preliminaries. Ignoring my salute and cheery "Good morning, Sir," he brandished a sheet of paper and glared at me over a pointed finger.

"I've got better things than this to think about. What the hell are you up to? Have you no idea what you've done? Can't you see the embarrassment?"

I had no immediate answer to this blizzard of angry questions, so took refuge in an upright, military posture and the traditional one-word guarded reply, "Sir?"

"Right, listen," said my leader. "You have invited a personal guest for tonight's dinner?"

"Yessir. He's ..."

"Don't you tell me who he is. I can read for myself." He waved the paper violently.

"Yessir."

"Why wasn't I told about this? The CO's hopping about and the Mess President has had to change everything at the last minute."

"But, Sir I did ask. You said it would be all right as long as I wrote a proper ..."

"Yes!" bellowed my distraught leader. "But you didn't say *who* he is, did you?"

"Well no, not then, Sir. But my notes did."

"That's the whole point, you damn fool!"

I was quite lost. Everybody had agreed that I could bring a guest, it was common practice and I would pay. He would sit with me and my colleagues. He was accustomed to formal meals and certainly wouldn't disgrace the affair by eating peas off his knife or whatever people were worried about. The boss was very upset. It was a puzzle.

"Now listen," he said in calmer tones. "You and I will have another talk about this tomorrow. Meanwhile do you know who is the only official guest tonight?"

"Er ... Um. Er ... The local police chief?"

"Precisely. And what rank is the local police chief?"

"Er ... Um. Er ... Chief Inspector?" It was a shrugged forlorn guess.

The boss grimaced. "Close enough. Your private guest is also a policeman, right? From what you've written, the President reckons he's something like five ranks higher than tonight's guest of honour."

"Yes Sir."

With weary patience my boss played his trump card. "Do you suppose the CO's going to let somebody that senior sit with you peasants at the bottom of the table!"

"Er ... No Sir."

"Exactly! The seating plan's been re-jigged. Your guest will sit beside the CO. To make things look right, God help us, you'll be on the top table too, but right on the edge. You will not put another foot wrong. Is that clear?"

"No Sir. That is, yes Sir."

As things turned out, it wasn't a bad night and the top table helpings seemed bigger than I was used to. My guest enjoyed it all and saw nothing odd in his placing at the table.

In the morning I reported to the boss as instructed. First on the agenda was the expected invitation to be available for extra duties. Then came the social post-mortem. "Well, lucky for you, it all went off all right last night."

The boss seemed his normal relaxed self, but caution beckoned. "Yessir."

"Yes. The CO's pleased and actually thought it was a nice touch to have two policemen from different parts of the country. I hope you didn't mention the last-minute seating change to your man. I don't suppose he noticed at all, did he?"

"No Sir, I don't think he did." Even if he had, I knew him well enough to know that it would not be mentioned.

After all, he was ... my father.

Making Tracks

~ 5 ~

Making Tracks

It was high summer, and I was a care-free young sprog without mortgage worries and similar matters which came as a plague later. On this morning I was also totally unaware that my commanding officer was making a routine inspection of his empire. These weekly rituals included a different area of the base each time and often resembled a royal progress of yesteryear. The CO took with him a retinue of anxious acolytes who were shown dust, unpolished brass, unchecked fire extinguishers and lazy subordinates. Some commanders were known to wear white gloves, the better to note dirty door frames and other neglect.

Suspicious wear was spotted on the grass between the gymnasium and the squash courts.

"What is causing that?" he demanded and, of course, an immediate and accurate answer was expected.

"What's that?" quickly demanded the descending levels of courtiers until, like Chinese whispers, the lowest airman present heard "Ooo the 'effing 'ell's done that?"

This man's sole task was to produce keys on demand. He was hung about with duplicates from the central keyboard and his jingling progress made the inspection party sound like a squadron of light cavalry on the move. He also gave timely warning of doom's approach. Now, safe behind his armour of lowly rank, his answer could not be denied. "Sah! Dunno. Sah!"

A fidgety silence ensued.

In the entourage was a diffident and normally unnoticed civilian whose role was to take note of the Great Man's horticultural likes and dislikes. He was usually completely bamboozled by important military matters-of-the-day such as bed-space hygiene and dry ration storage, but now found himself unexpectedly on strong ground. Taking full advantage of his moment he peered with dignity at the scars on the ground and in a strong voice pronounced his first opinion for as long as any in the group could remember. "These are tyre marks. I believe that some young officers cut across here on their bicycles."

"What!" cried the CO to whom the very notion of commissioned officers riding bikes was in itself incredible. "Never! I simply cannot believe that."

The grass expert retreated and bit his lip.

Around the corner at that very moment, mounted upon a slightly rusty government-issue steed, cycled your actual care-free young sprog, slightly late for duty again. No doubt, there was a proper drill movement for dismounting, but in the excitement of meeting my leader, it seemed simpler just to fall off. In a curious way the undignified scramble gave weight to the solemn proceedings. Grasping an up-ended wheel rim in right hand I saluted with the left

– nearly a hanging offence in itself – and stood to ramrod attention, bike clips and all, to await my master's pleasure.

At about six inches range The Boss gave a pointed assessment of my worth to the organisation followed by an irresistible invitation to accept extra duties on the following two Sundays.

Even then, two quite unrelated facts intruded.

Save one , the entourage suddenly found a lot of interest in the cloudless sky. The odd-man-out was, of course, the key carrier who memorised every detail with undisguised glee.

Then I noticed that the 'Old Man's ' razor could have been sharper that morning. It wasn't the time to say so, but there was a definite stubble.

However, only inspecting officers could remark such lapses and it seemed I would wait some while before acquiring that prerogative.

Does He Mean the Real Queen?

~ 6 ~

Does He Mean
the Real Queen?

The arrival of a new and vigorous commanding officer would normally cause few ripples to our pleasant life at junior level. We attended the first officers' meeting, of course, but even then listened with only half an ear while regretting the passing of another fine afternoon.

Things would be different this time.

In a long harangue our new leader first listed several areas where improvement was required – routine stuff for any new broom – and then announced that in the summer we would receive all of the Air Force top brass who in turn would host most of the Royal Family. Our Thames Valley idyll was to be the site of the 50th anniversary royal review of the Royal Air Force and even we recognised the career-limiting possibilities of that. The entire place, our commander assured us, would indeed be fit for a queen. Somehow it sounded very like a threat.

"Does he mean the real Queen?" whispered the back rows.

During the following months all came to pass exactly as the CO had foretold and those who were unable or unwilling to adapt to the new pace of life were found other more remote places to serve their country. Her Majesty would arrive mid-morning and be received by a full ceremonial parade and fly-past after which she and the attending party would take lunch in the Officers' Mess. A review of Royal Air Force activity would occupy the afternoon.

During this period a friend's untimely promotion saw me appointed as Officers' Mess Secretary in replacement and gradually this supposedly part-time duty took over my life as The Day drew nigh.

Priceless silver and paintings were sent by other units to grace the royal dining room. A lady assistant went 'through the motions' in the brand-new lavatory while checks for shadows were made from the nearby public road. I made endless notes for my immediate superior who, as President of the Mess, would formally welcome the Queen to the building and, of course, bear the cross of any failing. He soon developed a tendency towards twitchy checks on minute detail. This was entirely understandable as his normal place of work was on the ejection seat of a fast jet aircraft. We were all swimming in waters a long way over our heads.

The programme for the day was timed to the second and endlessly rehearsed. *At 1200 hours*, it said, *Her Majesty and the Royal Party is welcomed to the Officers' Mess.*

12:02 – Her Majesty and His Royal Highness withdraw. This line written with authority and in the sure knowledge that expensive works had produced separate retiring rooms for each. The twenty minutes which followed were vital to the plan. The Queen would go one way with her immediate retinue and the Duke with his, another. Meanwhile, the Air Force members of the cavalcade – all of them of rank beyond dreams – would receive perfunctory greeting from my harassed boss and, as confirmed by rehearsal, just have time to discard their swords and medals, relieve themselves and, as required by protocol, await the royal party in the reception room.

At this point I was to play a crucial part on the great day.

12:20 – Her Majesty and His Royal Highness are invited to sign the visitors' book in the foyer.

The book would lie on a fine polished table adorned with a delicate silver pen tray. Glittering crystal ink pots containing dense jet black and vivid red complemented the gleaming metal to perfection.

The Queen would use an antique silver fountain pen loaned by a loyal admirer, this to be properly filled with the smoothest black ink. Each rehearsal and countless anxious trials had proved the instrument's ability to write instantly. My job was to carry the pen next to my warm heart until the retirement, then lay it, suitably wiped and cap loosened, in its place on the table. I would then be about other duties out of the royal gaze.

There was a reserve, albeit lesser, pen.

A change of plan – and there were many – required the pen to be in place before the party arrived. An amended order solemnly advised:

Eleven fifty and three seconds – the Mess Secretary positions the Royal Pen.

This I duly did, only to watch my president, now in a fever of last-minute-trying-to-check-everything, take a scrap of paper to the writing desk. Needless to say, with all the perversity of inanimate objects, The Pen, still warm from my bosom, failed to write at once. A gentle shake – or even a little scribble – would probably have cleared it. Unfortunately, he at once dipped in the black inkpot within an inch of his hand; nothing could be more natural.

The pen reluctantly gave birth to a single jelly-like blot.

Immediately I made to retrieve the doomed Parker and reverentially proffered the warm substitute to my transfixed leader. Technical explanation was prevented by the next phase of programmed exactitude which had the royal motorcade rounding the last bend and thus banishing me from sight.

I had been too slow to prevent catastrophe, but recognised at once that confession would be unwise. Now he would never know that unauthorised experiments to create strong contrast between inkpot colours and the silver had been conducted. The red was a brilliant concoction of cochineal food dye while the impenetrable black was achieved by an equal mix of Indian ink and blackboard paint.

The whole day passed perfectly, but in the relieved euphoria which followed, it seemed best not to remind The Boss of anything and I sent the pen for restoration at my expense. Similarly, in the interests of consistent behaviour, it was kindest to allow the owner continued belief in the Sovereign's imprint forever carried by his pen.

I was only thankful that the repairers performed their miracle within a week and also that amount of pay.

Go To Biarritz - Do Not Pass 'Go'

~ 7 ~

Go To Biarritz –
Do Not Pass 'Go'

If the boss insists that you take an August weekend break at Biarritz what can you say? After all, it would be a working trip in support of the RAF parachute display team and might just clinch my position on the second reserve list of possible candidates for the stand-by pool for late selection to the team. Anyway, that was my story.

It was an entirely different matter to convince my wife, who was at that time mothering a small family whose combined age totalled less than 3 years. I could see her point. Biarritz for a late summer weekend in the name of duty was, perhaps, stretching things a little. My clinching argument, however, was that I needed to chaperone my great friend and colleague, David, who was almost certainly in line for selection to the team.

At Biarritz we were put up in the Hotel Regina, a magnificent fin-de-siècle pile all windows and indoor palms. Dumping our bags in a shared room, we quickly made a quivering return at the immense reception desk to receive our operational instructions. We were swept aside by a rush to the beach. Well, what could we do, but join in? The sun shone, briefings seemed a far distant event – if this was display parachuting, I could learn fast.

The team were to jump the following day at a nearby air show. Our role was to obtain a weather forecast, compare it with the actual winds measured by us on the spot and so give the parachutists highly accurate drop information. So, with about an hour to go, a puzzled French weather forecaster was quickly put at ease with rusty schoolboy verve in his own language. Unfortunately, while *la plume de ma tante* just about spanned my 10-year gap, the grateful boffin's burst of *atmospheriques et brises* defeated me at once and David's helpless laughter demonstrated that I would get no help from him. I don't suppose it occurred to us that the man might just speak English. The solution – as so often the case – was to take a look at the going conditions outside and simply embroider what we'd understood of the official version. Being August in Biarritz, the sun was shining in a windless sky anyway. The display leader seemed happy so it was time to get busy and make some actual measurements.

These were achieved by releasing a weather balloon with a known rate of climb and then at timed intervals measuring its angle to the horizontal through a surveyor's theodolite. Reference to a chart gave the drift and thus the wind speeds at 500 foot intervals. The balloon's rate of climb was established by inflating the thing with hydrogen until it just lifted a measure of brass weights. We'd done it countless times before. David was to squint through the telescope and my job was inflation, release and timing. An anxious period of hissing and fiddling in the back of our van eventually produced a magnificent eager sphere. However, when I released it – after a loud countdown for accuracy's sake – instead of sailing gleefully into the bright blue yonder in accordance with all previous advertisements, the bloody thing simply gambolled along the ground like a rebellious beach-ball. Only after an undignified caper and capture was it obvious that I'd forgotten to remove the brass inflation weights. From the team's view point – waiting in a flat calm to board the aircraft only four hundred yards away – it meant that by any drift and ascent table they cared to consult, a wind which carried the balloon horizontally must be at least 50 knots or more.

Between splutters David said that for the first time in his life, the expression 'off the scale' actually meant something and, wiping away tears of mirth for the second time that afternoon, he prepared to follow another ascent; this time without the weights. The boys just resigned themselves to the inevitable and, despite the expert assistance available to them, jumped with their usual immaculate accuracy, but it did appear as though my door to display parachuting had closed one more notch.

That evening, by way of thanks, the French Chamber of Commerce staged a huge banquet in another extravagant hotel and we attended as civic guests along with all other participants in the show. David and I, in keeping with our lowly not-quite-of-the-team status, took places at the bottom of a table – well below the salt. The main course ended with fanfares and flashing lights as teams of chefs proudly paraded confectionary *pièces de résistance*. To loud applause each table end reverentially received one master-piece. Ours looked like a fairy castle of the Disney school of architecture all topped by the three wise monkeys; see no evil, speak no evil, hear no evil. David, emboldened by the generous servings of wine and other refreshment, and far from his usual polished self, began to eye the sugary trio with intent. I was distracted by the announcement that our leader would reply in French to the municipal welcome and too slow to prevent David from snatching the cake's topknot and swallowing it whole. Unfairly, the figures were not candy, but some form of culinary plasticine which promptly filled the back of his throat with a rubbery plug rendering all speech and most breathing a thing of the past. Even though the fulsome oratory continued at the top table, I felt obliged to escort my mate on an elbow crawl across the polished floor and get him to the safety of the basement toilets. It was an errand of mercy, I told myself.

An evening in the Biarritz fleshpots was to follow and, as David seemed disinclined to take any further part, he was pointed in the general direction of our hotel and left to it – at least it was a warm night if sleeping out became his choice. In the early hours my return to our room revealed the chaos of clothes carefully hung on the floor and a comatose body which had missed both beds and the armchair. It seemed kinder not to disturb it, so an avalanche of blankets was the solution.

Later in the morning during my breakfast, David pain-fully recalled the kindly comments of a troupe of ballet dancers he had met in the foyer. Knowing nothing of ballet and, by that stage, even less of why he had come to Biarritz, he'd been unable to reply sensibly, though he conceded there may have been other reasons.

The return flight allowed ample opportunity to consider our future. For my part, someone who struggled to get a simple balloon airborne was an unlikely candidate for display stardom. David, meanwhile, having identified some bad tonic amongst his gin as the cause of his distress, vowed an immediate ban on mixers.

Only as we cruised serenely over the Channel Islands, did the immediate threat to our composure occur to us. With about an hour to go, we each needed to invent a story plausible enough to convince our sceptical wives – close friends, and bound to compare notes – that indeed the two duty days had been arduous in their demands upon us.

Thirty years down the line, I remain unsure if we ever did.

Let The Public See What They're Buying

~ 8 ~

Let The Public See What They're Buying

The musical pride of the Royal Marines, the jingling excitement of the King's Troop or the scarlet precision of the Red Arrows simply fill me with awe and I have the greatest admiration for the team members. In my own field an opportunity might have arisen to join the famous parachute display team of the Royal Air Force, except that I developed neither the skill nor the urge to appear in public. This probably dated from an early and unexpected brush with the genre.

Shortly after basic training I was to accompany an experienced and wise colleague to St Ives in Cornwall where we would liaise with a Royal Naval flying squadron and some troops of the Royal Marine Reserve. Their task was to demonstrate to the admiring crowds a beach assault. Ours was to control their preliminary parachute descent into the sea from a helicopter. The Green Berets would then board some inflatable boats and storm the surf line firing blanks from their rifles the while. All in the cause of gung-ho public relations.

The weekend's potential for interesting times began with the selected date of August Bank Holiday. Motorways were still points of argument in parish council halls, so our journey from Abingdon near Oxford took us via Swindon, Devizes, Frome, Glastonbury and, of course, the infamous Exeter bypass of those days. We shared the road with the entire holiday population of southern England together with their caravans. Our only advantage seemed to be the dull-painted Land Rover which was given ample space by the polished streams front, back and alongside. Ken, my mentor, calmly accepted all of this and drove serenely along apparently oblivious to the crush of the extended day. Memories after Exeter are vague, but we did eventually arrive at Culdrose, not far from St Ives, and were welcomed by friendly Royal Naval baths, horse's necks (a new drink to me then) and dinner. A man called Digby arrived during the meal. With a neat Vandyke beard and twinkling eye he resembled a modern version of Francis Drake. He was to be the pilot of our helicopter.

I sat at Ken's knee to learn while he and Sir Francis chewed over the morrow's task. There was the normal business of times and the like, but then new detail was discussed.

"Best get the vehicle there early," Digby warned. "You'll want to be right at the beach, but it's Bank Holiday, remember."

"How early?" countered Ken cautiously.

"Well, if you're any later than eight, you can forget it."

"Ah well," grinned Ken. "If there's a bit of a hike, my strong young assistant can carry the kit."

However, my vision of disagreeable pack-horse duty through the throngs immediately evaporated when Digby announced that the Marines were one parachutist short and would either of us care to make up the number? Ken reluctantly released me and promised to wait in the car park with dry clothing. All I had to do was parachute into the sea and get ashore with quiet dignity after the beach battle. No stealing of Royal Marines' thunder would be allowed and nobody would know that only five of the six parachutists were 'real.' Anyway, charging beaches rifle in hand was hardly Air Force work, was it?

The plan survived the night and until we were fitting parachutes ready to board. Ken had left for St Ives long before. Pole position in the beach car park was his aim. "Slight change of plan, old sport," announced Digby as I located my final buckle.

Hearing such news ten years later my cynical reply might have been, "You don't say?" On that youthful morning, however, an instant and respectful sharpening of attention resulted.

"As we've got the machine over the beach anyway," Digby explained, "I thought we'd let the folks see what else we can do. We'll put you into the sea from lower down."

Parachutists, even new ones, become suspicious when the word 'lower' is mentioned. "Er ... lower? ... How low?"

"Oh ... 'bout ten feet. You won't need a 'chute, of course. The crewman will see you all right."

Ten feet! Jesus! Come back soon, Ken ... please! Only seconds earlier I'd been happily contemplating a thousand feet or so, but TEN?

The pilot's cheery explanation of how the Navy put divers into the water from that height as a matter of routine was barely believable, but the short flight to St Ives gave little time for dwelling on the possibilities. With envy I saw my erstwhile colleagues depart under their parachutes and then clung on as Digby took us down in a steep swoop to rein the aircraft into a clattering hover. The crewman brought me into the door where, sitting on the edge, I thought I could just see the ocean far below. A minute boat drifted past, the upturned faces merely white blobs. "What height are we?" I bellowed.

The man grinned from behind ten spread fingers and thumbs. Bloody hell! What's the finger sign for the noughts to add to that? "Are you sure?" A thumbs-up confirmed the grins; it was time to go.

Much later Ken admitted that from the boat I did seem to be in the air for quite a while – perhaps the height might have been a little more than ten feet – but I was okay now, wasn't I?

I could hardly remember, because the next plan came immediately after my explosive arrival in the holiday town of St Ives. The battle for the beach had been won and to excited applause, the heroes were licking ice-cream and signing autographs. Digby still had his infernal flying machine in the vicinity and Ken came across to my rescue boat where I sat in wet, but relieved bemusement.

"Slight change of plan!" he yelled gesturing with the radio microphone. "They want to do a lift from the sea... You're it!" I was to be plucked out of the dinghy on a wire and winched into the helicopter to demonstrate rescue techniques. Ken's departing shout, "They'll lower you onto the beach," at least promised a more dignified second arrival.

Being fully trained in rescue I was able to grasp the wire as it came within reach and slip head and shoulders through the padded strop with confidence. The aircraft howled some fifty feet above and with a slight jerk I was in the sky again. Once suspended, it is impossible to do much, indeed the approved technique is to keep the arms extended firmly down the sides with the loop, of course, under the armpits. I was vaguely aware that we were moving towards the beach and above the machine's din, could hear faint echoes of an excited public address commentary. Half-way up as I began a slow twisting turn on the wire, the elastic waistband of my sodden track suit trousers give up the unequal struggle for that day. Taking my undershorts with them they collapsed about my dangling ankles at the precise arc of rotation facing the Bank Holiday crowd. From about forty feet and hoping the public enjoyed what they had bought, I displayed my all in the name of public relations and armed forces recruiting.

After a lifetime, the helicopter door appeared and the hard edge gave my bare bum a cold scrape as the near-hysterical winch operator pulled me in. Luckily, Digby judged the beach too crowded for a safe lowering and, from the wire again, but grimly holding up my rebellious togs, I was deposited gently in a space just beyond the beach. This allowed me to waddle in unobtrusively as if after a quiet dip and owing no connection whatever to the derring-do next door.

Ken's admiring comments were almost unbearable, but at least none of the crowd appeared to recognise the former dope-on-the-rope and in the back of the Land Rover I scrambled into dry kit.

"Please can we get going now?" I implored anxious to save something from the holiday weekend. I'd had enough of letting the public see what their taxes provided in the way of national defence.

"Ah..." was Ken's reply. "You see, by getting here so early I got the best position, but it's not technically part of the car park and there's about two hundred cars to leave before our exit is clear."

It is, of course, mere coincidence that nearly 20 years were to pass before I returned to St Ives.

Rites of Passage

Rites of Passage

Solitary occupation of a palatial office was no way to learn leadership and it soon became evident that closer contact with the workers, the men who really ran the show, would be an essential next step towards maturity.

My boss said that he had taught me all he knew, now it was time to enter the adult world of decisions and acceptance of responsibility. I could take on the health and welfare of older and wiser subordinates. Each one, he warned, would be happy to watch their green new leader cover himself in... in...

"Well, you'll just have to see."

An early task was simple in concept, but required a lengthy journey over the Libyan desert which in that area resembled the heaps of road grit to be found alongside major roads in England. My team comprised a lean stripped-down Land Rover full of assorted expensive equipment and an equally lean, but fully dressed sergeant called John. He was rangy in the manner of cowboy film heroes, and favoured a habitual grim expression complete with laconic delivery. He was known, however, as a fine instructor and also for his awareness of the environment which pre-dated by a long way the 'green' revolution. My friendly, but nervous chatter was simply ignored and as we left base, I was uncomfortably aware of his reputed dislike of all officers on principle.

Within minutes of leaving the coast road I was lost so, after some moments of furtive fiddling with map and compass, invited my scornful but silent companion into democratic consultation.

"How the hell should I know where we are," he muttered. "I'm not the bloody officer, I'll just make some tea."

Even in my innocence I recognised it as a first test, but was careful to make no rebuke. After all, he was the only company I was likely to have for a couple of weeks. Crestfallen squinting along a bearing and a murmured "Awfully good tea, John", saw us under way again, and that night, alone in my officers'-only tent, I pondered the mysteries of how such beverage could be produced from thin air.

In the morning we established a post on high ground overlooking our operating area which proved to be an extensive tract of brittle gravel seemingly no different from any other. Our role was to attract low-flying aircraft which appeared at regular intervals to drop things onto us by parachute. We used cloth panels of violently coloured fluorescent green and orange to construct a huge signal letter on the ground which the approaching pilots would see from miles away.

One day after a couple of drops and the usual radio taunts of the cool, clean crews in their air conditioned machines, we retired to our pile of stones for lunch and shade. John limited the conversation to sardonic opinion on the aviators' parentage – all officers apparently – but produced tea at the normal high standard.

Our vivid signal remained clearly visible to a casual glance, but it appeared diminished somehow as distant hands acquired the latest trend in Western dressmaking material. With some diffidence I asked John to abandon his meal, take the Land Rover and safeguard the remains from the invisible thieves. To my relief he left without argument – things were looking up – and returned shortly with a much-reduced bundle of colour and an ancient Arab who brandished a rusty rifle. This worthy had greeted John with a mime of chasing off the culprits and now claimed his reward of a box of rations. It seemed like a locals' confidence trick even to me, but it is amazing what a firearm can do for understanding the other fellow's point of view. Smiling with the front of the mouth whilst muttering through the side was a new skill.

"Do you reckon that thing's loaded? Let's have a look and make sure."

"Nah," scoffed my protector as he gestured imperiously to the old man, "just look at it. That thing couldn't fire toffee."

To our surprise the gun was proudly delivered to my hands without protest. Although it appeared to be made of driftwood, galvanised gas pipe and copper wire, faint etchings in the metal betrayed better days. When it 'broke' shotgun style, a sweaty cartridge could be seen in the breech. Suddenly, the owner snatched it back and with a gap-toothed grin, swung about as if on a demented grouse shoot.

There was no explosion, but John ducked convulsively and literally bit the dust. I suppose I was just too innocent to react quickly enough. "Bugger this for a game of soldiers," came a muffled judgement from around my ankles. "Let's give him some grub."

"You do that, John. I'll make some tea."

Years later, mellow in his final months before discharge from the service, John towered over me at an all-ranks party. "Yeah, Boss, I suppose you didn't turn out too bad in the end..." He swigged his beer and I basked in a blush of accomplishment. "For an officer."

"But, Christ!" he shook his head sorrowfully. "That bloody tea!"

Dinner With The Colonel

~ 10 ~

Dinner With The Colonel

Once upon a time a young RAF officer was astonished, but privileged to serve a short tour of duty with a battalion of the Parachute Regiment based as garrison on the island of Malta. A Soviet heavy cruiser anchored on the northern horizon appeared as the only threat to peace, but as strategic considerations were well above his pay band, he could simply lie back in the sun and think of wintery England. Because he was an attached 'Blue Job' his day-to-day masters, unsure of Air Force custom, tended to let things be. His real CO was 1500 miles away. Shamelessly exploiting the best of both worlds, it was a rare state of bliss for a young man.

I was that officer.

It was meant to be a short stay – "Just have a look and report back", the boss had instructed. There was a hint, however, that conversion to a full tour could follow, my wife and children would come out and we'd all enjoy two years or so in the Mediterranean. The RAF appointments branch disagreed, however and insisted that it was not my turn for such a perk. This angered the Army who had decided that as they liked me well enough, then so should I stay. A medium level argument ensued and a two-week stay extended into a second and then third month.

Most of my work involved catching a freight aircraft on its circuit around the Med. I would get off at a grim airfield called El Adem not far from Tobruk and vanish into an area of Libya seemingly the size of Wales. There I would eventually make radio contact with a parachute dropping aircraft, we'd agree the day's plan and do it. The clean, well laundered crew would return to base and I would crawl into my sand-filled sleeping bag with a tin of rations until the next day. After a couple of days or so, I would return to El Adem like some latter-day Lawrence of Arabia, thumb a lift back to Malta, have a bath and then ease into the brandy sours at the Malta Hilton. This latter I considered to be the very front line of national defence.

And still my fate was argued. In a letter my wife informed me that the younger of our two tots had forgotten who I was. Could I please send a recent photo. The end of month three came nigh.

I was, of course, a full member of the battalion mess and indeed made most welcome. Nevertheless, it was important to remember my status of guest, albeit working for my supper, and I was careful not to offend regimental custom. It mattered not a jot that The Paras were some 20 years or so younger than the Royal Air Force. My colleagues, often former members of other, older formations, were indelibly steeped in ancient tradition. Dire, but heroic disasters such as Arnhem inspired their military ambitions. They were charming, but not really interested in the Battle of Britain. Furthermore, they had to a man endured considerable hardship to acquire their red parachute beret. I thought myself tough, but by their standards was only an average member of a somewhat effete organisation which wore pale blue as uniform. This latter hardly a match for the drab hair-shirts of the ground forces. Their tolerance was that of a gang of street urchins being followed by a persistent but harmless younger child.

I knew my place.

The mess was undergoing refurbishment that spring, so our public rooms were compressed into one place separated by folding screens. Before dinner one evening the 'young gang ' – I had won my membership – were in fine mood and, as I finished my drink, the others went round for the meal. Looking for continued fun I performed an impromptu 'Punch and Judy' show with one hand over the screen top. "Ectoplasm! Ectoplasm!" I warbled wiggling my fingers disjointedly.

A complete and crashing silence greeted this effort. A second turn was absorbed as if down a deep mine shaft.

A protesting rush around the screen, "Come on, fellas! What's? ..." ran me into a barrier of beautifully cut light tweed. The battalion commander, an awesome lieutenant colonel of airborne troops, had come unexpectedly to join his juniors for the evening. Now he regarded his idiotic guest impassively.

I took my place at the end of the soup queue.

In the edible silence our steward seemed to mime his service; not a single clink.

Surrounded by his majors and captains the colonel took his proper place at the table head. Below them the subalterns took their places rank on rank. It was clear where I should sit.

Left thumb strictly in line with the seam of my slacks, right hand holding the bowl in the approved manner, I took my place at the foot of the table; 12 short feet away from the great man.

Exceptionally polite soup-drinking noises followed until, at last, Colonel Peter looked directly at me.

As if by parade-ground order, all spoons were lowered.

In deep misery I awaited the thunderclap.

"Tell me," he said mildly. "Has the dear old Air Force decided when you will leave us?"

Good Night, Ma'am

~ 11 ~

Good Night, Ma'am

The fine red-brick manor deep in the Shropshire country-side was actually a Royal Air Force group headquarters and one of the last examples of a more gracious style of military life. About 20 of us served there under an amiable survivor of fearful wartime derring-do, for whom every peaceful day must have been a bonus. Our function was to give direction to a group of stations which happened to be on the other side of the country thus allowing leisurely drives when visiting. Between times we lived in charming family style fully in keeping with our surroundings where it seemed entirely proper to gather in the elegant drawing room for morning coffee. Gradually we educated our subjects not to bother us with telephone calls between ten and eleven.

Being least in rank, length of service, specialisation and age I served many masters and because badges and insignia mean a great deal in the armed forces, had quickly learned the vital skill of the 'rank glance'. This counted badges on first meeting and so established at once the pecking order of the moment.

It was a simple rule. More stripes than you – defer eventually: many more stripes – much more deference, and quick about it. A look to the left breast also assisted professional intercourse for here were found pilot's badges and the like and, more importantly, any war medal ribbons. A longer, more admiring gaze was permitted in this direction, especially if some former gallantry was recorded and so an instant CV could be divined.

My new chief carried the four stripes of a Group Captain together with a multi-coloured war service pedigree, but I took care not to gaze too long at the rainbow bosom. You see, my new leader was also and undeniably a woman. Things are different now, but in 1969 very senior female officers were few and I had certainly never been so close. After a hesitant start when chauvinism vied with career survival, I warmed to her style and gradually began to bask in the glow of her occasional approval. I retain happy memories of being towed along in her wake as we inspected dining halls as part of a competition and being met by anxious catering officers with gallons of 'G & T' and "he will have a beer." She was, and in many ways remains, the finest officer I have ever worked for.

In the relaxed surroundings of the headquarters, personal relationships had a chance to blossom a little, but on one formal dinner night her direct order, "You! Into the loo with me, now..." brooked no argument. In the best traditions of obeying the last command I exchanged my evening clothes and we emerged from separate cubicles into gasps of astonishment immediately followed by cheers of approval. My sky-blue cummerbund and monkey jacket just about covered her majestic upper works. Her grey shirt-waister dress fitted me comfortably and at half-calf length revealed regulation black socks and shoes. We bowed and curtsied to our delighted commander whose aide was reduced to a jelly of protocol anxiety as he pored fearfully over the guest list.

All in all, I considered that my career was being done a power of good and when my wife and I were invited to our first tennis party, stardom beckoned. Tennis parties meant whites and Pimms instead of ordinary clothes and bitter. Nobody left the bar and while there might have been some racquets and balls lying about, I can recollect no actual play. It was at this first and only occasion that I risked the growing support of my patroness.

She was in good heart and I basked in what I fondly supposed to be our 'special relationship'; after all, we really had swapped evening clothes. In a bold move a couple of personal thoughts from Junior seemed in order. Two Pimms later was the moment.

"Do you know what I think spoils the womens' service?"

"No I don't, young man. Do tell," the faintest chasm yawned behind her smile.

It should have been a little badinage between familiars fondly recalling past campaigns. I should have recognised the signs. I could have feigned sudden sickness, a fainting fit, even my turn to serve in the non-existent doubles match, but... no.

An expectant hush awaited my pronouncement.

"Well... Well... I think it's this awful ugly word 'Ma'am' for senior ladies. I'm sure that a better word could be used."

She towered over me, overwhelming in her presence and other features. "Oh so you do, do you? Well you know well enough what to call me, don't you?"

"Er... Er... Yes, sir... That is, Biddy... I mean Group Captain... Oh hell! – Goodnight Ma'am."

Eat This Message
After Reading

~ 12 ~

Eat This Message After Reading

"What are you like at keeping a secret?"

It was that quiet question from the boss which told me this was it. Everybody knew that MI5 recruited from keen young officers and I'd often wondered how the moment would arrive. What a good job I'd had my new jacket cut loose. Just right for the shoulder holster.

The small unit where I'd spent the last two years was to disband and a rump of the staff remained to hand over our function to other establishments, see off the last of the beer and then close the place. I was the junior by many years, and a few ranks, so my days passed in daily whirls of 'now do this', 'go there', 'see to that.' Until, that is, my leader's oblique reference. Now my eyes X-rayed the room for electronic bugs. "Secrets, Sir? Pretty good actually." This was not the time to confess that routine signing of the Official Secrets Act at cadet school had frightened me half to death, especially as I'd had no idea what it meant.

"Good oh," he said. "Your next job is to report to the classified documents registry and witness the destruction of it all." My heroic dreaming had obscured the twinkle in his eye.

And that is how I found myself in a windowless room in charge of a first generation paper shredder which sounded like a very old washing machine on economy wash with a couple of house bricks. All around was a positive rainbow of coloured document files, terrifying secret red, intriguing confidential green and boring old buff-coloured ordinary. No Miss Moneypenny, however, and no improbable gadgets dreamed up by 'Q'. It might well have been Her Majesty's Real Secret Service, but James Bond it was not.

Most young men of my tender years in the service never held the awesome responsibility for a single page of such national importance let alone be allowed to read it. Now, on my first look at the shadowy world of state secrets, not to mention bravely fighting off the hostage-takers, the boss was telling me to tear up the lot.

I would not be entirely alone. My Bond Girl was the calm civil servant who had run the classified document registry for twenty years. She had never mislaid a single item and did not appear to be a target for the baddies either. I worried over her relaxed efficiency and saw the closely packed files spelling the end of my new career. I never knew secrets existed in such numbers. In my mind I reviewed vaguely remembered definitions of disclosures to the enemy which may be harmful, very harmful or extremely prejudicial to the interests of the nation. Just to pick up the red covers seemed to burn the fingertips and set the alarm bells ringing in Whitehall, or perhaps with the Queen herself. No wonder spies are licensed to kill; a minimum of life-imprisonment would follow the loss of a single paper clip.

Even so, it was all very strange. Normally I had only occasional access if needed in the course of my duties – a most unlikely event – but the clerk was fully authorised to handle the stuff on a daily basis. Now only I could mark its destruction. Another puzzle was that once the files were signed out for shredding, they became my responsibility until the certificate of destruction, signed by me, was duly put away by the clerk in a document registry which had ceased to exist. Suddenly I could see where John le Carré got his plots and began to cultivate a nice line in tight-lipped stealthy behaviour.

Most files bulged at around one hundred carefully numbered letters and other bits of paper. Some had clearly been the subject of much grubby-thumbing, but others had clearly passed straight from the envelope to the file – unread and lost for ever. I remembered with dismay that the inclusion of only one secret document was enough to raise the classification of the whole file to that level. A solemn count of contents was compared to the existing index on each file, the clerk removed paper clips, pins and string tabs and then fed the individual sheets into the shredder's maw. Agonised munching then produced high-quality hamster bedding in the bin below and I developed eye ache through trying to watch the progress of each sheet.

After my companion had smoothly fed the beast without sleight-of-hand for some while, she announced break time as the next test of nerve. Far from just locking the door for a twenty-minute break, the only way open to my level of experience was to follow the regulations exactly and perform the entire rigmarole of counting, signing and returning everything to the locked document store which, of course, I was in the process of destroying. I cannot imagine what she said to her colleagues, but my coffee was ruined through worrying about SMERSH getting at the sacks of shreddy left upstairs.

This level of paranoia could not last and on the second day I was persuaded by amused wiser colleagues that the woman should be trusted. She had, after all, been running the classified registry since before I began at junior school. Further, I was advised, things would speed up a bit if tea breaks and the like did not invoke the full majesty of the Act. Matters should then have proceeded apace except that on the third day the clerk's new appointment was effected immediately leaving me to complete the job alone. I was assured that a special licence allowed me to witness myself unlocking, counting and destroying.

The level of responsibility was fast overtaking my pay-band and now included removal of paper clips and other bits of indigestible debris which littered the files. Losing bits of paper, even when shredded, was one thing, but negligently giving the machine the wrong diet was the more heinous crime by far.

By day four the sheer monotony of it all ensured that even the most intriguing secret barely raised an eyebrow.

A chance sighting of my own training report had me reaching for the cyanide pill again, but into the jaws it went and I felt slightly surprised to remain in one piece. A head-nodding production-line developed. Pick up the file. Compare its title to the destruction certificate. Sign off the slip. Remove the metal work, bits of string, pressed flowers and old railway tickets. Try for two or even three sheets at a time. Admit defeat when the shredder choked. Clear the blockage. Try not to breath too much of the paper dust which soon filled the room. Oh yes, it was high-risk espionage all right.

I reasoned that if every item of paper, classified or not, was destroyed there could be no mistake. So in went the fire evacuation instructions from the back of the door, the machine's operating booklet and yesterday's newspaper. By the end of the week every dread secret in the place had been reduced to ticker tape and I was left with several large paper sacks brim full of the stuff, a heap of mangled paper clips and a hot mincer.

With a real sense of having foiled the enemy it was time to collect together the destruction certificates, one for each file, all witnessed by my signature. These would be catalogued and sent up to the grander, even more secret lodgement of our controlling headquarters. In the absence of the clerk they would prove that rather than selling my country for a few pieces of silver, I had done my duty clear of eye and straight of back.

Of the certificates there was no sign. Not one. Only their heavy card clip files remained.

A frantic rummage elbow-deep in the nearest sack revealed the truth. Below the top layer of finely torn newsprint and amidst the twisted remains of red, green and buff appeared the occasional thread of orange. They matched exactly the well-remembered, distinctive shade of the printed certificates. In a moment of grasping hope I wildly fitted two or three strips together to see if any words magically appeared. Bond might have an answer, but not me.

As things turned out, the closure of the place was too close for my masters to concern themselves and my confession became something of a joke as we saw off the last of the bar stocks.

Even so, for some months into my new appointment I expected a visit from the heavy brigade in trench coats and snap-brim hats. "We're trying to trace a few files of secret documents," I knew they would say, heavy with menace. When no such call came I began to relax a bit until one morning my new boss got me going again.

"Hey, the paper-pushers are in a flap up country. They've lost all their secrets."

"Er, how's that, boss? Is there a problem?" Heart rate off the scale all of a sudden.

"Well, not for us, but didn't you hear the news? Their headquarters burned to the ground this morning. Nobody's hurt, but there was so much bumph in the place it went up like a torch. They've lost every record for the whole group. What a laugh."

So Who Is Bill Then?

So Who Is Bill Then?

Despite modest rank, I found myself for a while well up the pecking order of the RAF Sailing Association and was to be the sole light-blue representative on the racing committee during an annual inter-service regatta on the Solent. The previous year had seen me arrive in my vintage wooden yacht from which I had rowed myself ashore complete in yellow wellies and scruffy sweatshirt – but then I had only been a spectator.

This year was to be different. Properly turned out in formal slacks and blazer, I presented myself at the King's Steps in Portsmouth Dockyard to board the Naval ferry provided to take all committee and competitors across to Seaview on the Isle of Wight. Low tide prevented close approach so a shuttle of boats and launches of decreasing size was used to ferry us ashore. The competitors simply waded the final few yards, but the committee was reverently escorted in small yacht tenders by a wet acolyte on either side. And so, feeling somewhere between the hero of 'African Queen' and a 'D' Day veteran, I arrived dry shod at the host yacht club.

Proudly assuming my role as RAF Representative on the committee I climbed at once to the club balcony there to meet various officials of the other services all dressed as I was and all anxious to perpetuate the rigorous traditions of Solent yachting. The introductions proved that the Navy and Army had different views of the occasion and I was outranked in all directions by several degrees. All, that is, save one very affable soul who, dressed in comfortable casuals, introduced himself as 'Bill...' As one frequently does on these occasions I missed the surname, but 'Bill' seemed appropriate and so it continued.

Quickly discarding my blazer and tie, I seemed to gravitate naturally towards him and while the others made important decisions of procedure appropriate to their retained dress, Bill and I happily messed about with flags and minor support tasks.

During the afternoon word went around that no less than The Queen's Harbour Master was to visit the event and that indeed his barge had left Portsmouth. My new naval colleagues were quick to point out that the title, Harbour Master certainly did not describe the usual brand of retired mariner who took your money for a night's berth. Nor, for that matter, could his splendid vessel, now in gleaming view, fit the usual description of 'barge'.

He was a Royal Naval officer in an appointment of no little influence hereabouts and as he approached, a little excitement was aroused amongst the gathered hierarchy. Ties were straightened, flags triced up and a committee member of considerable rank scuttled down the slip to receive the visitor. After a fine show of boat hook drill by the barge crew, the Queen's Harbour Master was landed and escorted with some deference to the club. Ties were adjusted once more, tea arrived in silver service and I even found my discarded blazer. Bill, however, appeared quite unmoved; did he not understand the eminence of our approaching visitor?

As this latter stepped onto the balcony, however, I was baffled to note a decided change in his demeanour. He appeared to diminish strangely and to have eyes for one man only. What is more, although they appeared to know each other, he was most obviously deferring to my new friend. I stepped aside while the escorts formed an admiring group around.

So who had I been exchanging not-too-polite lower-deck repartee with all day? Who was the amiable Bill who had tolerated my juvenile descriptions of the rigours of service life with sympathetic nods?

Panic-stricken and before the introductions reached me, I fled to the club office desperately searching for my list of who's who in service sailing circles. I had at least worked out that Bill was in the navy, but what? But who?

Ah, here we are... page 24. Admiral Sir William...

Just the Harbourmaster's boss-in-chief, not to mention a sizeable part of the Navy... That's who.

At the end of the afternoon it seemed best to take the public ferry home.

Gonged Again

~ 14 ~

Gonged Again

"Right," said the Boss. "Let's give the programme a final look in my office."

It hadn't been much of a day, a dull Friday during a not-too-bright summer. We all seemed to have too much to do and the annual inspection by the group commander was as imminent as next Tuesday. My commanding officer, determined not to be caught unprepared by a change of itinerary, had insisted upon frequent checks on cleaning progress. This meant that I had spent most of the week nagging Mr Jo, the luckless Warrant Officer whose job it was actually to get the work done. Eventually, satisfaction was conceded after a final walk-about and approval given to stand-down. It was just after five thirty and I was to meet an appointment 100 miles away by eight. The 'final look' shouldn't take long, I was ready to go and knew the road.

That plan was immediately modified by the sight of the Adjutant getting out glasses and bottle as we went through. Good, I thought, a tot for Jo and his deputy. No hard feelings and we can all go home to wipe the slate clean for next week. So five senior and junior managers crowded into the Boss's inner office.

"Aye," says this latter, clutching the bottle in a fierce Scottish grip. "We'll no be needing the cork," and the stopper spun off behind the filing cabinet. As a survivor of similar declarations, I sensed that my 'Plan A' for the evening was already at 'Plan B' and began to compute latest departure times against maximum intake.

At this point the Boss thrust a battered letter at me and then went the rounds with the bottle. His timing was perfect and, at the last glass, I was able to announce, "Gentlemen, the CO's been awarded an Air Force Cross in the Birthday Honours List." I knew then that the sailing club meeting all those miles away would simply have to get along without me. As his deputy I owed him absolute loyalty and, besides, there was the matter of the unfinished bottle to consider. He went the rounds again exchanging handshakes for more whisky and amidst the clink of refill there was a smacking of lips, broad grins of anticipation and much leg stretching as everybody settled in for the night.

My goodness, that bottle went quickly. Luckily there was another in the outer office and it was at that stage that I thought to warn my long-suffering partner. Conscious of misusing an official telephone, my message comprised curt sentences of regret for yet another ruined meal and the late return which was certain to follow. I had to be quick, those blighters were already well through the second bottle. That lasted only marginally longer than the first, but a search in the safe produced a supply of 'visitors' sherry' which would keep us going until reinforcements arrived.

These were brought by our leader's wife whose husband clearly had no inhibitions over telephone use. Luckily for him, her verbal thrashing was diverted by the arrival of a group who had been working late elsewhere. Attracted by the din, they had intended 'just to look in', but their grinning anticipation caused Mrs CO to beat retreat leaving the bottles behind. More corks joined the others behind the cabinet and the new arrivals quickly settled into the spirit of things with plans to bring in crates of beer and chips from the Sergeants' Mess. All that is, but their chief who quickly claimed that he had a meeting to attend about 100 miles away. Clearly, and despite his junior rank, he possessed faster wits than I, and he was seen to pour the famous brew into the hard helmet clutched under his elbow.

Memories become a little vague after that. I recollect that our commander's wife made another vexed appearance; was there another bottle? The meeting-man escaped before the whisky dissolved his hat and the rest of us were at the war-stories stage. Mr Jo, was a former RAF boxing champion and still displayed the inscrutable menace of an Easter Island statue. He told us how good it felt to connect a strong right cross and watch the opponent's eyes glaze as the knees buckled. That revelation produced a moment or so of relative sobriety as we gazed carefully at our feet and silently thanked our various gods that the man appeared to be on our side just now.

Worried that practical demonstrations might be next, I made preliminary moves to leave and broke the silence with the clear announcement, "I shtill hash thash meetin togettoo. The wyfelltek me." After several misdialling attempts I got her to understand that I would be awfully glad if she would come to collect me and we'd leave my car at base. When she arrived we were in the middle of another bottle, more unlikely tales and beginning to wonder what it was we were celebrating anyway. Out in the car park I faced floods of tears. "Washer hell's rong now?"

We were all in a dangerous occupation at that unit and, after years of awaiting fateful phone calls or uniformed padres coming long-faced to the door, the poor girl had feared the worst after my terse initial message. She had imagined another fatal accident, possibly to a close friend, and her relief at the real reason for the delay was just too much.

It was my sympathetic concern which brought down the thunderbolt. "Well at leash you knew it washent me!"

So Saturday was another bunch-of-flowers-with-head-ache day and not for the first time I asked myself. Just how do the women cope with it all?

Bouncing Along

~ 15 ~

Bouncing Along

School days had taught me that to play with honour was the most important aspect of sport. Such naivety, however, was no preparation for the peripheral demands of a sporting weekend in Lincolnshire some 20 years later. My job was to arrange a summer games weekend between my service college and visitors from the Royal Navy.

The signs of an interesting weekend in store appeared early on the Friday morning.

"Hallo, mate, it's me," phoned my opposite number in Devon. "We're at Newton Abbot station and should be at Grantham on time."

"Great," I enthused. "The bus will be there." Then in a moment of light-hearted banter. "Don't forget the trophies."

"What trophies? There's no trophies here. See you."

"Hang on, you won last year, remember? Hello... Hello..." The phone simply echoed the miles between us.

I was an indifferent sports enthusiast really, but, thanks to a loyal expert staff, had provided a billiard table cricket wicket complete with freshly varnished stumps to receive the impact of vividly waxed leather balls. The mobile score box, prised out of the nettle bed, gleamed in fresh green paint. Rafts of cucumber sandwiches and real Earl Grey tea would appear at the pre-ordained moment. Not far away bleached spectator benches surrounded a whole Wimbledon of tennis courts. Boxes of snowy-white balls, rackets, eye-shades, umpires' high chairs, squash and ball-boys were all timed to parade exactly to the minute.

All the teams had to do was face up in competition on Saturday and may the best one win. This was especially so for our own gallant players who needed to avenge the heavy defeat inflicted by the Navy last year. I had done my bit and could rest easy to enjoy the spectacle.

The horde of bronzed young men at Grantham railway station looked little different to our lot and there was my old friend again. "Good to see you. Fair journey? Hope the trophies didn't get dented."

"I told you on the phone. No trophies, and I mean it."

All prospects of a swift recovery from this disaster were delayed by our immediate invasion of 'Happy Hour' back at base. We all mingled, drank beer, swapped boasts, then blazers and generally indulged in a hour or two of serious limbering up which included a sporting meal of sausage and chips served at the bar.

After some while our commandant's aide, still in uniform, appeared in the crowd. He was a tall, lugubrious soul of sad dignity entirely proper to his appointment. "Hello there! Have a beer." I welcomed loudly. "This berk," I continued, poking my naval guest, "has forgotten the trophies."

The aide left abruptly, but returned almost at once. "The Commandant would like a word."

I had a length of corridor and a grand staircase to straighten my blazer, clutch at my hair and prepare a defence. I'd been given no hint as to what the great man wished to discuss, but I knew. Oh, yes, I knew. No amount of faultless preparation in other matters would disguise the fact that there was a lack of gleaming silver. On the plush carpet I received a succinct invitation to resolve the problem forthwith and heard the hope that this would be the sole deficiency. I passed the remainder of my evening in the silver room urgently searching for a couple of anonymous pots to grace the prize table.

On a calm sunny morning the cadets took to the field in immaculate whites only matched by the starched brilliance of the umpires' coats, the green of the wicket and the polished sheen of the spectators' chairs. After an hour's cricket the crowd comprised myself, one of my staff and a man walking his dog. To my dismay the Commandant arrived. "Good morning, Sir," with an eager leap to feet. "The Navy's in bat. Twenty five for one. What a lovely day..."

"Never mind all that. Where are the spectators?"

"I, er..." Visions of busy supermarkets and car washing crowded in. "I feel certain there'll be a good turnout this afternoon, Sir."

"Well, let's hope so for your sake. What time does the tennis start?" It was not the moment to remind him that he held the carefully printed programme in his hand.

After a moment's bristling silence the Commandant left, but was replaced almost immediately by his deputy. This was the man I really needed to please as he was my day-to-day chief. " Good morning, Sir," there were a lot of *Sirs* at this place. "The Navy's in bat. What a lovely..."

"Why is their flag bigger than ours?"

I gaped and, sure enough the flags bravely adding colour to the scene were indeed different in size. "Well... er ... umm. That's our usual one, Sir. Oh! Good shot there," and I tried some short-lived applause.

"It may well be, but you've not answered the question. See to it, will you." He turned to leave, "and there's a litter bin with a dent in it over there."

Unnoticed, the cricketers played on.

"Okay, Boss," sighed my own deputy. "I'm sure there's a bigger one in the shed." He gestured towards the offending cloth, easily the size of a good-sized bedspread. "Bert ironed that one last night specially, you know."

It appeared that our groundsman was a more sure-footed politician than I.

And so, bigger flags flew, polished bins sparkled and spectators eventually grouped themselves here and there. We won the tennis, they the cricket and the Commandant presented the borrowed trophies one to each college and to the satisfaction of all.

The next most important matter of the programme was to be the grand dinner and party during which all sides would fraternise and swear eternal brotherhood. Thankfully, I was not a cook.

Dinner was splendidly lively and afterwards we staff repaired to the bar in company with about a hundred fighting fit young men in their early twenties. The Commandant's aide advised me that his man and immediate entourage would make a brief token appearance later.

A chance comment heard in the general inter-service hubbub warned me that the Navy were about to mount a spoof parade and would march in bearing one of the squadron colours hanging in the central rotunda. These had been laid up with the full tradition of regimental colours in a church and were virtually religious icons. Only with great difficulty did we persuade the young idiots to let them be. Nonetheless, despite the imminent arrival of the Commandant, we were unable to prevent a broomstick and towel flag being slow-marched through the bar by a straight-faced colour party. They stepped sideways in honour of the Navy's affectionate name for we of the RAF. Prancing slowly like the crabs they said we were, they shoved our astonished leader aside and, accompanied by a drunken comb and paper band, solemnly stamped the length of the main corridor.

The Commandant's party turned and left at once, leaving me to review with deep gloom the most likely remote spot for my next appointment.

According to my plan, all agreed by the Navy, Sunday was easy. We knew the train times for Devon, so the bus was booked for a full two hours before. Breakfast would be a moveable feast for two further hours before that. I would count heads, sign the driver's job sheet and wave farewell on behalf of the RAF.

Five minutes before the planned departure, I had one eager bus, but only two rather sickly passengers. A car with a flag on the bonnet appeared. It was the Commandant. All those present jumped about a bit. "Morning!" He snapped crisply. "Ready to go? By the way, what the hell was going on in the bar last night?"

"Good Morning, Sir. We seem to be a bit short of Navy just now. Excuse me, I'll just check on breakfast." As I scuttled away another car drew up; it was the Deputy Commandant. I was suddenly thankful to have dressed in well-pressed slacks.

The breakfast room was empty of both Naval and Air Force youth, but a slight trickle of groaning creatures began to board the coach. Not one acknowledged the bristling RAF brass. "Look here," menaced the Deputy Commandant, taking me aside. "The Commandant's on his way to church, you know and your programme clearly said departure at ten. Why isn't it?"

Thirty minutes later we awaited only a few stragglers and, as my leaders marched crossly about the place, I was glad to have allowed for unforeseen delay. At last, the final latecomer arrived. He was the senior naval visitor and spotted my master at once. "My dear Commandant," he boomed, grasping a reluctant elbow. "You fellows certainly know how to lay on a party. Absolutely splendid. I feel ghastly!"

He boarded the bus, I counted heads. We all waved farewell. "Don't forget the trophies next year!" shouted my opposite number.

My summons on the following morning had a fearful inevitability. I was not invited to sit. "There were a few areas needing attention," began the Deputy Commandant. "You must remember how important detail is on these occasions. Take the flag, for instance."

"Yes, Sir, I do see now," I muttered, my mind reeling with images of small, un-ironed trophy-shaped crabs.

"And to have the Commandant waiting beside the bus was simply not on. You must look after our visitors properly."

"Yessir."

"Well, you've some way to go. By the way, remind me of the cricket score." I passed over my immaculately typed result sheet, saluted and turned to leave.

"One other matter," I stopped in mid-stride. "We quite like you really... You bounce well."

Will This Do?

Will This Do?

Of the many instructions I had given, the latest could hardly be described as inspiring.

"Well," I said in my best I'm-in-command manner. "The tower can be seen from the motorway, so when we do, just steer for it." The driver knew me well enough to give a slight snort of disbelief, but otherwise kept his eyes firmly to the front.

We were on our way to Windsor Castle and nearly two miles down the road, before realising that neither of us had even been to the town, let alone the castle. A telephone call the previous afternoon had started things.

Our unit was about to receive HRH The Prince of Wales as a student on our parachute training course, with his brother Prince Andrew arriving for the same purpose a week earlier. It's not that we were in state of panic – indeed most plans had been well laid – but, as the training officer responsible, my mind was in permanent overdrive.

"Please stand by for a call from Buckingham Palace," warned a distant operator the day before.

At that stage of play, such a call was not entirely unknown, but I came to a wary state of alertness while an officer with a name sounding awfully like a full page from Debretts, required me to attend on Prince Charles tomorrow. He wished for us to give him some preliminary training in how to make parachute landing rolls.

"Tomorrow? Okay, no problem." What am I saying? Prince Andrew arrives next week. Next week!

"Jolly good," said the dark brown voice, so obviously unused to contradiction. "Ten o'clock, then. At the castle. Good bye."

Only the click of disconnection prevented me blurting, "Er... which castle is that, then?"

I was due to feature in a formal inspection on the morrow, but my boss graciously conceded that of all the unlikely excuses for not attending, being ordered by the Prince of Wales to Windsor surely was the most imaginative.

My disbelieving driver that morning was the sergeant instructor who would actually manhandle royalty during the training. He was a tough Welshman called Glan and his derision over my navigation was entirely understandable; I could hardly claim to have my mind on the road.

Our surprise at how adjacent Windsor High Street was to the castle entrance was quickly replaced by wide-eyed amazement as we were whisked through a succession of gates and arches where the police guards appeared to react to some form of invisible signal. Feeling like tourists who'd lost their way, we pulled up alone in the private ward of the castle and were greeted by an impossibly elegant figure. Our heads told us that he was really a manservant, but, as he looked like a fifth earl at the very least, our hearts insisted that we give him an impeccable parade-ground salute – just in case.

By way of a creaking mahogany lift we were escorted into Prince Charles's private rooms and abandoned. Neither of us dared say a word, but rather listened to our mounting heart beats, while resisting the urge to inspect the framed photos on the desk. Our student-to-be soon appeared, however, ready for work in military combat dress. Prince Andrew suddenly arrived similarly attired and the spacious room seemed a trifle small somehow. He had many enthusiastic questions to ask, but was quickly silenced by his elder brother.

"I expect we'll need somewhere to work," observed Prince Charles and led us off at a fast canter into a maze of corridors, stairways and halls. Each area was immaculate and I wondered how our collection of dusty rubber training mats would fit in.

Eventually we stood in a vast hall where display cabinets sparkling with orders and decorations stretched a glassy floor into infinity. My failing grasp on reality was only restored by the incongruous sight of a ladder propped behind the gigantic entry door.

"Will this do?" asked our leader, eyes twinkling.

Glan had said little so far, but now surpassed himself. A brief glance around. "Yes, I suppose so."

Our modest car could be seen beyond the massive windows and we went off to lug in the mats. As if out of the ground a couple of men arrived to help us. A third man in a kilt appeared and somehow the whole business was becoming a little unreal. Together we laid an area on the glittering boards and work began with Glan, now resplendent in perfectly pressed overalls, bullying the two princes around the rubber. His crisp commands and cries of encouragement echoing around the roof beams brought a succession of courtiers to a distant door. They seemed to be checking on the well-being of their masters and withdrew with a slight bow when satisfied. As if seeking a comfort blanket, I found myself looking at that ladder from time to time.

"Enough! Enough!" Puffed Prince Charles after a brisk half hour or so of parachute rolls. They had both demonstrated better-than-average ability for beginners.

We returned at a fast pace to the apartment.

Now with portable screen and slide projector, it was my turn. Pictures of what awaited Charles and Andrew during their training course was to be morning's *pièce de résistance*.

I had a slick, well practised script for this visual feast. It had been an oft-repeated part of my preparatory work throughout the planning stage, and I knew that the slides were neither back-to-front nor upside down. The screen was quickly in place and the princes sat expectantly. I was humbled by Glan's open-eyed loyalty; after all, he'd seen the show almost as many times as me.

My casual reach for an electrical socket was immediately followed by a more panic-stricken search; not one was obvious. A ludicrous compulsion, dredged from some half-understood protocol brief, prevented me from turning a sweaty back as I forlornly swung the projector's plug.

Common sense suddenly switched on and simply following the flex from a desk lamp led me to the outlet. Only seconds had passed, but it seemed that an unforgivable gaffe had been perpetrated.

The slide projector had a perfectly normal 3-pin plug of the type found in any semi-detached home of the realm. Very obviously Windsor Castle was not in that category of dwelling and, try as I might, the plug refused to fit. Very soon The Prince of Wales joined the struggle, but Glan gallantly restrained the youthful exuberance of Prince Andrew with a burst of parachute training techno-babble.

Surely, I prayed, a secret bell would summon a footman who, armed with pliers, would save me from The Tower. "All is not lost," grinned Charles. "Let's just hold the things up to the light."

And so, with great good humour, he did. "It won't be like this on the day, Sir," I claimed dejectedly as I hopped about muttering disjointed bits from the script while peering over the royal shoulder to see the transparency.

Prince Charles's grave reply carried a hint of warning, but the twinkle remained. "I am sure that you are correct. Thank you both for coming."

The kilted man was absent for the car loading, but a couple of footmen appeared presumably in response to another esoteric signal. Sweating through exertion and anxiety we set off.

It was my turn to drive, but within seconds the car was surrounded by noisy crowds who peered in excitedly. There seemed to be no way through and like caged animals we circled round aimlessly until the throng thinned abruptly where an ornate iron gate barred the way. Beyond we could see the rigid back of a red-coated Guardsman and then ordinary Windsor town life proceeding heedlessly.

We probably outranked the sentry by several degrees, but there seemed little prospect of persuading him to open up for us, so it was back to the crowd and more anxious circuits until an exit suddenly opened and we escaped. The mystery of the crowd's sudden appearance was only explained later when we learned that many of the Royal Family had gathered at Windsor that day to attend the Confirmation of Prince Edward. They were not really interested in the two famous instructors at all.

On the motorway, Glan at last vented his true feelings.

"Pheweee!" He produced an enormous cigar – the sort brought out by film stars when sons are born. "Permission to smoke, Sir?" he gasped.

"Feel free," I granted. It would have been churlish to refuse, for his part had been faultless. "I think we did all right there," Glan was already disappearing into an expensive blue fug. "Everything will be okay on the day."

However, I mused, future equipment for visits to royalty had better include an electrician's tool bag ... and a proper map... and a set of those towelling cuffs tennis players use to mop the fevered brow... and I'd better have another talk to the protocol people.

On the other hand, when my masters enquired of progress, an airy assurance of well-being might be best.

Blame The Weather

~ 17 ~

Blame The Weather

To be a weather man must be the worst of occupations. No matter what is forecast, somebody will be displeased and there's no control over events anyway. During some of my service it was important to cultivate good relations with the local weather men so to ensure immediate and sympathetic attention to the impossible demands of our task.

In 1978 HRH Prince Charles was to pass through our parachute training system as a student and *oh, by the way,* the planners said, his younger brother would come along too. I happened to be the training officer at the time, so my masters were obliged to accept that perhaps under close supervision I might just carry off the task without ruining the dynasty.

Even so, many non-specialists seemed to be convinced that certain death, or at best disabling injury, awaited the heir. If that happened, I was solemnly assured from behind barricades of detailed and largely incomprehensible written orders, a sparsely furnished room awaited me in the Tower of London.

There were benefits, of course. One had only to whisper 'royal training' for unprecedented support services and equipment to rain upon us. One of these was to be a mobile meteorological team attached to me from our headquarters. To my surprise, the civilian weather forecaster I knew from previous occasions and who normally favoured crumpled slacks and Hush-Puppies, made his first appearance completely booted and spurred in camouflage combat clothing.

Any doubts I harboured concerning his team's military worth were quickly dispelled when a full weather station sprouted from the back of their van. This came complete with chart printer, wet and dry thingummyjigs and all surmounted by a lightweight mast bearing an assortment of expensive gadgets of extreme delicacy. This wand was rigged with a maypole-like skirt of cordage supporting it in every direction, but increasing the ground area twenty fold. It would, however, produce meteorological data of minute and immediate detail. All-in-all, it was a huge improvement on throwing tufts of grass into the air and holding up a wet finger.

As the great event approached, the excitement grew apace and all save my staff and I seemed to be getting into a fine old froth. Even so, and to my dismay, we were required at the eleventh hour to prove that our field was big enough to accept descending royalty, so a full dress rehearsal with other parachutists was arranged. Everybody would play their part including the met men who were especially pleased for the opportunity to calibrate their instruments well before the real test.

On the practice day a series of delays left me somewhat short of time for calm travel to the dropping field. Other considerations such as thinking about the weather, setting the ground signal and establishing communication with the aircraft would all be affected. Soothing other fevered brows and remaining fully in command would, of course, be taken for granted. The consequent wild dash through the Cotswold countryside did nothing for my assistant's nerves who loyally bounced around in the back of the Land Rover clutching his wits and other bits of equipment. It was necessary to remind him that we at least must remain in complete control of all strings to be pulled. Professionalism was everything.

On arrival, weather was first on the list and we quickly spotted the slender mast with its attendant soldiery. With a final stern injunction to my harassed aide to be careful and not to go kicking through the supporting cords with his great boots I pulled up close by the met station with élan and protesting brakes. The weather mast's rigging appeared to be growing from the side of the vehicle and, as the engine noise ceased, there was a curious twanging noise from under the wheels.

What I had intended as an immediate and much-needed assumption of command was entirely upstaged by the instrument pylon which, relieved of most restraint, gracefully bowed as if in welcome and deposited its crown of expensive and delicate gadgets all over the wet and dry thingummyjigs.

The instruments abruptly lost all interest in further proceedings and no amount of frantic adjusting by the anguished weathermen could save the situation. "That's all right, Sir," they gritted bravely. "Luckily, we've brought our bit of sea- weed. Ha! Ha!".

Quietly I slunk back to base to report that proving of the royal parachute dropping zone was postponed that day as impossible weather conditions had intervened.

Who Tells the Microchip What to Do?

Who Tells the Microchip
What to Do?

Increasing age and seniority should bring along protection from the self-inflicted tribulations of youth, but events in my personal fortune ensured that Nemesis still lurked at every turn. After a lifetime of being 'hard to tie down', I found myself 'flying a desk' in an unvarying nine-to-five daily routine. I was unprepared by training, background or inclination for the appointment, so the opportunities for innocent error were legion. There was also the matter of a coincidental if belated introduction to the computer age.

A 'station management system' was installed which comprised a central computer linked to individual work-stations all over the unit. It resembled a rather dull air conditioning unit with no sign of the dramatic reel-churning, light-flashing dominance embedded in my expectation. I could see the need for a warm and dry lair for the thing, but why so brilliantly lit night and day? There seemed no answer to this naive question so I concluded that the electronic hobgoblins did indeed emerge from their rather dull cabinets to squeak and click the night away.

Naturally, I convinced myself that I was no laggard in this magic and, fooling no one, relied heavily on experiences from a previous station where advanced computer studies were a part of the task. There my keen mind had pestered the experts with the endlessly repeated question, "Who tells the microchip what to do?"

Patronising laughter and metaphorical pats on the head would be my only answer. "Never mind," they would splutter with superior grins. I would retreat to my more robust duties of teaching young men how to polish their bed-space, run around the gymnasium and march about with head up and arms swinging.

So now, and feeling like a persecuted character from *Nineteen Eighty-Four*, I warily returned the screen's impassive gaze. Although linked by man-traps of coiled wire to keyboard and printer, I told myself that it was only a glorified typewriter. Then I remembered that in more complex mood it could speak to the beast in its comfortable den along the corridor. Before long, however, the mere process of switching the thing on each morning, involved such a trail of unlocking keys and remembering random-letter passwords that I would frequently delay the effort. My secretary would then remind me that vital 'E-mail' – another mystery – could not be received and I would be out of contact.

E-mail was then best retrieved by stepping the few paces to my CO's office and, over morning coffee, receive my daily orders in the time-honoured manner. We were of an age, entertained similar bewilderment and expressed mutual sympathy. We also felt the irony that having just reached sufficient eminence to warrant a personal assistant, it seemed possible that soon she would be replaced by a machine.

"Can you get the cricket on yours?" The boss gave the rectangular eye a meaningful look.

"I'm afraid I cannot even get the test screen yet."

A demonstration that neither of us was giving our new tool the respect it demanded.

We shamelessly exploited the 'help-line' which connected directly to the civilian providers of the equipment. They would send down a delightful young woman, fully-qualified to deal with the ineptitude of middle-aged buffers, yet retaining the long-legged freshness of feminine youth just like the old days.

"Try things out," she would encourage.

"If only..." we would sigh dreamily as she left us to the mysteries of the user handbook. Written in a curious Japanese shorthand, translated via Californian sales copy into technical English, it was completely unreadable.

Our PA endured a frustrating week or two with little to do while we exhausted the novelty of processing words in all directions, but soon it was time for a few experiments with the 'mainframe', as I had learned to call the cabinet in the brightly lit room along the corridor. These trials would be utterly private, I decided, so when the CO was on leave, our surprised aide was sent off for the afternoon.

My appointment code allowed access to the deepest personal records and I was amazed how quickly my own number, rank and name could be displayed. This led to discovering how many children I had and since when. My wife's full name appeared and – lo! – she shared the same address as me. The power and all-encompassing memory of the creature was awesome; how had we managed without this magnificent equipment?

Let's see why my tough policeman neighbour was so coy about his middle name... Clack, clack, clack went the keys – this is fun – the screen cleared and reformed and ... My goodness! No wonder.

Well now, how many days leave has my immediate subordinate had this year? ... Clack, clackety clack. What! As much as that? I must be getting soft.

The machine helpfully prompted greater recall of information and soon, as confidence grew, it was time to try the printer. This was fuelled from a cardboard box by a thick wad of paper folded back and forth like a fairground steam organ's music.

The rules required that only my own details should be printed and I was amazed to see that these comprised several pages of detailed information on long forgotten events. The innocent question 'PRINT YES?/NO?' also appeared. This was new ground indeed. For the first time ever I was to possess an authoritative printed record of my service life to date. There could only be one command – 'YES'.

The screen gave a single surprised blink, but not one inch of that carefully folded paper passed through the inert printer. Electronic *rigor mortis* prevailed.

I typed the command again. The screen winked at me once more, but continued its firm statement that I was English by birth, over half a century old and did not own a house. The printer sulked in silence over its paper meal.

No amount of button-pushing, paper-adjusting or swearing could persuade the damn-fool bloody machine to do my bidding and I was forced to read the instructions on how to revert to simple word processor mode. Turning it off from there was easy and I went home happy in the knowledge that the limits of computer knowledge had been pushed back a notch or two.

In the morning I was met outside my office. In itself this was unusual – my people tended to scuttle away first thing until the day's mood became obvious. This man wore a helpful badge identifying him as the Computer System Manager. He carried a large cardboard box identical to that which lurked under my useless printer.

"Good morning," and indeed it was.

"Er, good morning, Sir. Could I have a private word?"

The PA appeared with the ritual coffee. "The System Manager would like a word..."

"So I see. If that's a paper refill he's got, it's too early. I've yet to persuade my printer to work."

"Well, Sir, it's not exactly that..." Then with something of a gulp, "Was there a special reason for requiring the records of the whole station last night?"

While I gaped at him, coffee cup in suspended animation, he revealed a few yards of the box's contents. Folded paper, just like steam organ music, detailed in close print every recorded fact about each one of the thousand or so souls on the unit. I guardedly confessed to limited experimentation. The boffin continued in as simple a language as he knew.

"Well, Sir, your job gives you unrestricted access to all records?"

"Of course."

"The machine knows this, recognised your code and spilled the beans as you asked."

"But, bloody hell, only my own details!"

"Yes, but a previous command wasn't cancelled and the entire record was searched."

"So why didn't my printer do its stuff?" This with all the conviction of the self-educated. "I'd have noticed then and turned it off!"

"Well, Boss..." A suspicion of an indulgent smile. "The order was too big for your workstation, so the mainframe recorded the demand in its memory and waited for one which could cope. That was the big machine down the corridor and it's been working flat out since two o'clock this morning."

My only response could be humble apologies and a promise to destroy immediately something like 100 yards of wasted paper.

"Not to worry," said the manager. "That printer never gets enough to do anyway. It's nicely bedded in now."

After he'd gone I called my PA.

"Anita, we'd better have a slight change of morning routine. Coffee on arrival as usual, but I'll leave the keyboard work to you as it used to be. Is there a dust cover for these machines?"

Put it There, Norman

~ 19 ~

Put it There, Norman

Amidst gloomy, rain-soaked fells and the dour grey walls of an Argyll farm the modern bungalow was an incongruous beacon. Lured by its welcoming lights, I was left with no choice but to ring the door bell. A weak whirring then a second, firmer press produced a shadow dimly seen through the frosted glass. It shouted back into the house. That's when I should have run for it.

I'd been on the road for a couple of weeks or so, making a succession of surveys and land measurements stretching from North Lincolnshire to the very south of Kintyre. It had all been in delightful country populated by lovely people, but it was time to turn south and head for home. At midday I quit my spartan accommodation at the military airfield near Campbeltown and had one final task to complete. A quick chat with the landowners, possibly a call into the local police office, an hour's sprint around the peat hags and I could be away by tea time. Two hundred miles of hard driving – say five and half hours – could see me at Moffat almost exactly opposite to my starting point. Another fifty to Carlisle before tiredness and common sense forced a bed and breakfast halt. Then a daylight rush down the M6 to Oxford and, with luck, I'd only lose half of my first day-off for weeks.

Finding the lane leading onto the moor was the easy part, but the jagged pot-holes of the track soon exposed the limitations of a saloon car. Tomorrow I may well rush joyfully down the motorway, but today, the absence of my Land Rover, would call for a muddy foot slog, map and compass in hand. The airfield had remained in hazy sight at the turning; perhaps I should have obeyed my instinct and returned to borrow a cross-country vehicle.

The hard-worked Cavalier was soon abandoned in what appeared to be a roadside quarry and I made my way on foot towards the roof tops of a sizeable farm just showing above the throw of the land ahead. Dressed in olive drab combat clothing, I probably became invisible immediately to any watcher. Not that any were apparent – only keening birds and a soughing breeze – but I could not allow the peace of it all to distract me, it really was time to go home. A couple of hours should see this through.

Not one of the buildings showed the slightest sign of recent habitation, except that tucked away off the stone-flagged yard was the bungalow. I rang the bell twice and saw the figure. "Ooo!" I heard the shout. "It's a soldier. I like soldiers."

Everything screamed at me to melt into the increasing gloom, but I was transfixed by a beaming smile atop a diminutive tweedy outfit. In Oxfordshire I might have heard "Yeees?" or perhaps "My husband's in the back with the rottweiller." Here, however, the destruction of my good intentions for that day was immediate. "Come away in," she said and threw wide the door.

"You'll be taking your heavy boots off," only confirmed my fate, so in not-too-clean army socks, I padded through into a desperately over-furnished room where the heat closed about me like a trap. "I'll be putting the kettle on just now. Here's Alec, he's had a little sleep the while."

In centre stage a dusty armchair contained a further mound of tweed which gave heaving birth to a rusty face. A ragged cuff separated from the heap and gave faded green eyes one brief swipe. Immediate speech was switched on. "Aye, what's your name, Norman?"

"Well, actually it's not Norman. I'm called ..."

"Oh aye, Norman, you'll be taking a taste." Late, far too late, I noticed the bottle at his feet. As if by conjuring trick, a large tumbler appeared beside the one already on a side table. The bottle joined the glasses – clearly this was a formal occasion – and, as they darkened to the brim, I realised that my Scottish host held no truck with the alleged parsimony of his race. "Aye, aye, aye," he sighed piously and raised his glass in salutation.

Just in time I realised... It was the toast... We drank... I gagged... My watering eyes strove to read the label. Again too late, he had taken a grasp on the bottle neck as if to prevent it escaping. "Aye... What's a soldier about here?"

"Well, actually I'm Air Force, I'm just working with the Army for a while. I'd like your permission to walk across the..."

"That'll be the English Air Force... Aye," he nodded wisely as the woman arrived with a gigantic brown tea pot, what looked like the Sunday-best china and a plate of fruit cake slices each wrapped in a skin of pastry. Such had been my father's favourite complement to strong whisky and I recognised for certain my doom.

"Aye, woman," greeted Alec with warmth. "This is Norman. He's a soldier in the English Air Force."

"Well, my name's really... Er, thank you."

He was brandishing the bottle again. Both hands were now fully occupied with tea cup and whisky glass. "Er... thank... Whoops! Just a small one. I've got to..."

"Aye, aye, aye." I drank and during further splutters, dimly perceived a huge paw extended as a friendly hand shake. "Put it there, Norman," he commanded.

Only a psychologist would have noticed that it was the tea cup I set down to take his warm, but surprisingly soft grip. "Aye, aye aye," we drank again. As an act of visitor courtesy I filled my cauterised mouth with cake and tea and noticed that Mrs Alec, whose actual name was not to be revealed it seemed, had taken up a glass. Oh dear! dear! dear! Like a glittering claymore, the bottle waved again... "Aye, aye, aye." I had noticed that local custom clearly demanded a fill to the brim for each raising of the glass.

"What's a soldier in the English Air Force, aye doing in the Air Force, Norman?"

"No! No!," scolded my hostess. "He's just wearing soldier clothes. He's in the Army's Air Force really. Isn't that right, Norman?"

"Um... Well, you see I really belong to the Air Force, but I work all the time with the Army just now and I'm looking for some land for parachuting." It was the longest speech I'd managed since entering.

"Parachuting! I used to have a parachute," squealed Mrs Alec and without warning, scuttled from the room.

Alec seemed not to notice. "That'll be the English Air Force," he affirmed. "Put it there, Norman. Aye, aye aye," and, as if practising variations on a theme, we drank over the unbreakable clasp of eternal brotherhood. My neglected tea cooled on its table.

The lady of the house returned bearing a wide photo-album which she triumphantly threw down before us like a carpet seller. "There. That's me!" she cried.

I was astonished to see a recognisable slip of a girl in World War Two flying kit – and parachute – standing before a bomber aircraft of some sort.

"And there's me again. And here's Alec in his Navy uniform when we got married. He was in the Navy. I used to take the new aeroplanes from the factory to the aerodromes. Alec was a sailor then."

The book was full of similar photos – all from the war – and I was staggered to realise that she'd been a ferry pilot and Alec the skipper of an armed trawler. How they'd got together was a mystery I'd rather not explore.

"Aye. That was the English Navy," said Alec with feeling. All glasses were drained again for the memory. "Aye, aye, aye."

"Well," I attempted, after a few reflective moments. "I'd better make a move and walk the moor before it gets too late. Is that the track outside..."

"Oh! Your tea's all cold, look," and she bustled out.

"Aye, aye, aye," Alec and I agreed. I'd only just noticed that the bottle was twice the usual size and we had a way to go. Escape was impossible, we were shaking hands again. "Put it there, Norman."

"So do you like being in the Army, Norman?" enquired Mrs Alec serving fresh tea.

The conversation turntable seemed to be speeding up dangerously.

"Well, I'm really in the Air Force..." I began again.

No clock was visible in the room, but it was definitely darker outside and meanwhile I was losing track of time and much else beside.

Alec had been dozing in the chair, but suddenly broke in energetically.

"How much you got? How much money have you got?"

Carefully I felt my loose change.

"Well, I suppose I've got about ten pounds on me all told..."

"No! No! How much in the bank?"

"Er... Um... Well... Er. If I sold the car, I might just about raise a thousand pounds."

"That'll be English pounds, aye," he mused. "Put it there, Norman. Aye, aye, aye," and in a fraternal grip we took the holy water again.

Suddenly, throwing his arms wide, he encompassed the whole house, a dark block of pine trees barely visible through the windows and the countless square miles of dank Scottish moor.

"For that money, it's yours ... you can have the lot!" he grandly declared and then abandoned us for abrupt slumber.

Mrs Alec calmly accepted my chaotic protests that I really must... and how lovely it had been. Soon, clad in cold boots again, I took an unsteady stumble in full darkness down to the car. Not only had my land survey crashed on take-off, but I was in no fit state to drive anywhere, let alone Carlisle. Retrieving toothbrush only, I stamped myself half-sober along the couple of miles to the airfield where an impassive sentry gave me an immaculate salute as I ducked under the barrier. Presumably it was normal at that place for solitary officers without luggage to stagger damply out of the night.

"Hello, Sir," grinned the mess manager. "Back again? You can have your old room."

I turned to go with dignified thanks. "By the way," he continued, "you won a prize in last night's bar draw. It's a bottle of malt whisky."

He held out his hand in congratulation, "Well done, Sir! Put it there."

What's Water Got To Do With It?

What's Water Got
To Do With It?

After a lifetime each of military service in various parts of the world with not a few dangerous moments, Douglas and I were brought together in the autumn of our careers to share the same dingy London office block. We faced our final enemy in the shape of the last word in office computer equipment. It was known by the acronym CHODE and would, so we were assured, give membership of the trendy new club of the electronic office. It was going to be the death of us.

Thanks to years of battering a portable typewriter, I claimed to understand at least the logic of a keyboard, although could never have explained it to anybody. The letters were simply on certain keys because they'd always been there – don't ask me why. Douglas, a long-time, albeit cultured, action-man, was still at the one-fingered hovering stage. Often a hesitant search for a key would produce any letter permutated at random from the entire board. The resultant drafts frequently resembled a one-off cypher message straight from a spy film. Luckily, as we were not expected to cover for the other, I could listen to his swearing next door with a clear conscience. In truth my supposed superior knowledge was ephemeral and we were both innocent babes in a wood full of bytes.

It was a curious thing that while we wrestled with our perplexing machinery a fully staffed typing pool awaited our command upstairs. They even had wands to wave over a handwritten document which, by some optical magic or other, would absorb our scrawls directly onto the screen. From there it was a simple matter to translate our words into perfectly formed print. This could then be returned to us in something called 'hard copy' which seemed to be the new word for paper. The alternative was the touch of a single button to transmit the whole lot directly to our desk. As we'd yet to master reliable button touching of any sort, it was hardly surprising that the girls enjoyed many hours doing cross words while their highly-paid masters did their job for them and not too well at that.

After a month or so of my arrival and just when binary light was dawning, an improved system replaced the old. Douglas's protests were only muted when he saw that the new keyboard appeared identical to the one he'd nearly come to terms with. He'd progressed to two, sometimes three-finger operation and gaining confidence daily, so wondered what was special about the new equipment. The only thing immediately obvious was the inclusion of an elaborate system of interlocking security checks. We learned that progress towards a usable screen was only possible after the operator had passed each stage. Failure at any one would deny access to the next and the machine would simply not let you 'in' .

"Who the hell wants to be in?" was my friend's grumpy comment. "The bloody thing's just a tool. What do you think?"

"Well, I agree, actually. But then sometimes I never turned my old one on anyway. The Boss always nags about it when he wants to send an e-mail message."

"He's only across the corridor! He could shout."

There seemed no answer to that except that we were clearly in danger of being side-stepped by progress; the CO had a similar machine at home apparently. Douglas and I agreed to pool our knowledge on the first occasion of trying to get in to the new screen; we would use his office.

The first obstacle was that the electrical socket was guarded in a locked box supposedly to prevent snoopers simply plugging in and typing away. Doug said he had the key around his neck on a string. Repeated groping followed by near nudity failed to produce either string or key so we had a cup of tea and contemplated this latest set-back to our computer education. After a while a root about in my desk drawer found a key for my box and it worked on Douglas's. We'd passed the first hurdle.

A piece of plastic resembling a credit card had next to be inserted into a slot. This was unique to the machine and also to the operator whose appointment code it carried. It was supposed to be stored in a combination lock security box also on the wall. To open this mini-safe involved an infuriating sequence of dialling numbers to the right and left alternatively. Just remembering the correct order was test enough. Stopping at the mark with the right one each time was a cruel exercise in self-control. Douglas had the sequence written on the back of his watch strap. Some times he didn't wear a watch; today, thankfully, he did.

"Read them out," he commanded, taking off his time-piece before advancing on the box with malice afore-thought.

"Five right, forty-five," I intoned from his Timex.

Douglas dialled five.

"No, not five. The first number is forty-five."

"Arrrr! Bloody thing! Are you sure?" and the dial began to spin hesitantly through our incantations.

The final code. "One right to zero," I advised with a sigh. Just as the nought turned to the top, Douglas sneezed, the dial jumped and the entire lock rescrambled itself to secure. I went for more tea to the strains of muttered "Five right, forty-five." It was going to be a long day...

An angry shout brought me running. The opened box gaped at us and we peered into it like incompetent cracks-men. There was no card. Nothing. Silence ensued until Douglas, fishing suddenly in his hip pocket, triumphantly produced a warm plastic rectangle.

"Just testing," he grinned. The machine eagerly gobbled up the card despite a distinct bend from Doug's back pocket and, after a moment of fizzing, the screen flicked on blankly. Another step forward. What was that word? ... In. We were nearly ... in.

On the well-tried principle that if all else fails, read the instructions, we turned to the books again and learned that the machine now required a sight of Douglas's appointment title. Confidently he typed it in and this appeared instantly on the screen. Success. Only an hour after starting and we actually had something readable in front of us. The last step, we were instructed, was to insert a six-letter pass word. This, together with all the other checks would convince Chode that a meaningful relationship could ensue.

"Okay," said an excited Douglas. "I've already chosen a password. It's *SQURTY* but I'll have to kill you now 'cause you know my secret."

"*Squirty?* Squirty's got seven letters, it's spelled S-Q-U-I-R-T-Y. It means jetting water or something like that."

Douglas was looking angry again. "What's water got to do with it? It's the name of the keyboard, stupid."

"Keyboard? The keyboard's called *Canon* – there, look." Then, realisation dawning, I fell on his shoulder in a friendly gesture of brotherly sympathy. "You're thinking of a *qwerty* keyboard. It's the name given to most standard keyboards, including typewriters. It's spelled Q-W-E-R-T-Y after the six top left keys."

Douglas took my affectionate touch as deeply offensive patronage of the afflicted and, as occasionally happened in moments of stress, he reverted instantly to our former relationship as my commanding officer. His leadership style was forthright Caledonian which now appeared at full strength.

"See here, you Northumbrian bumpkin," he prodded, eyes narrowed, "it's my machine and if I say it's *SQURTY*, then why can't it be that? What do you know anyway?"

In his frustration, however, he'd forgotten that I had since been promoted and now enjoyed equal rank.

"Oh well, in that case, *Sir* [with heavy emphasis], you can switch your own bloody thing on. I've got one of my own next door!"

An international incident was only averted by a plaintive bleep from Chode which then informed us that several aeons of computer time had elapsed since our last action. Furthermore, save immediate action on our part, the system would turn itself off in three minutes and counting. Douglas eyed the screen warily.

"What do you suppose that means? I'm being threatened by a plastic box now! Come on, you. Think of something. You're the typist. Anything but that bloody combination lock again!"

Although friendship was again cemented in the face of the common foe, the long impassioned speech had used many precious seconds. A frantic flip through the book revealed a two-key code which could cause a choice of randomly selected six-letter groups to be displayed. Choose one of these to be your final security hurdle, type it in after clearing the screen and Bob's your uncle, or techno-babble to that effect. None of the winking letters spelled Doug's personal choice, or indeed, any word in English.

"Hey, what's happened to old *SQURTY* then?" I crowed, then fled for more tea as Douglas again reverted to clan chief. Just as the kettle boiled, more enraged bellowing, this time with a hint of despair, had me rushing back to our tormentor.

"I've typed in a word and sod all's happened," wailed Douglas. Sure enough, a blank screen stared contemptuously around the room.

"Are you sure you typed properly?"

"See you, Jimmy," he growled theatrically. "Read the book for yourself."

The screen smirked at us while we flapped through pages of electronic double-Dutch and then announced a renewed period to shut-down – still counting. At last, in small print the patient text explained that to foil prying eyes the six-letter codes were received, but never appeared on the screen. Doug's chosen code had really been there all the time. He wouldn't have to kill me after all.

He pressed the 'enter' key – we even knew some technical terms now – the machine gave a discreet burping note, the screen blinked a couple of times and proudly displayed a choice of functions. That we understood none of them, was quite beside the point. It was enough to send us jumping around the room punching the air as if we'd just won the Nobel Prize for Physics.

Just then the office manager, a man who wrote with a pencil on one of those outdated clip-board things, put his head round the door.

"Sirs," he yelled above the happy din. "There is a gas leak downstairs. I have to ask you to close everything down, lock away all keys as usual and leave the building as soon as possible."

My erstwhile leader, suddenly showing all the signs of Rob Roy McGregor on a bad day, reached for my throat. It was time to leave. Who was I to disobey standing orders for building evacuation? Besides, my machine was safely locked away next door...

The End